Table of Contents

Theology of the Seven

The Catholic Apologist's Handbook

by

Dr. ant

Copyright 2024 Dr. ant. All rights reserved.

No part of this book may be reproduced in any form or by any electronic or mechanical means including information storage and retrieval systems, without permission in writing from the author. The only exception is by a reviewer, who may quote short excerpts in a review.

Although the author and publisher have made every effort to ensure that the information in this book was correct at press time, the author and publisher do not assume and hereby disclaim any liability to any party for any loss, damage, or disruption caused by errors or omissions, whether such errors or omissions result from negligence, accident, or any other cause.

This publication is designed to provide accurate and authoritative information with regard to the subject matter covered. It is sold with the understanding that the publisher is not engaged in rendering professional services. If legal advice or other expert assistance is required, the services of a competent professional should be sought.

The fact that an organization or website is referred to in this work as a citation and/or a potential source of further information does not mean that the author or the publisher endorses the information the organization or website may provide or recommendations it may make.

Please remember that Internet websites listed in this work may have changed or disappeared between when this work was written and when it is read.

Theology of the Seven: The Catholic Apologist's Handbook

Contents

Introduction

The Catholic faith, with its rich tapestry woven over two millennia, stands as a beacon of timeless truth and divine mystery. Like any enduring edifice, its foundations have been laid meticulously, stone by stone, by leaders, saints, and countless believers whose lives and writings offer a compelling invitation to faith and reason. This introduction seeks to set the stage for a comprehensive journey into the core of Catholic understanding, grappling with its profound teachings, and inspiring those who approach it with skepticism or inquiry.

The heart of Catholicism is its faith in the Triune God, expressed through sacraments, scripture, and tradition. The Church doesn't merely propose a set of beliefs but offers a profound encounter with the divine, aimed at transforming both individuals and societies. This encounter is at once mystical and rational, a dual path that has engaged some of humanity's greatest minds and souls—from St. Augustine's introspective confessions to Aquinas's soaring philosophical treatises. Each argued that faith and reason, while distinct, are harmonious—two wings on which the human spirit rises to the contemplation of truth.

Catholic apologetics, therefore, is not merely defending a set of religious precepts, but an invitation to an expansive dialogue where faith seeks understanding. This approach offers believers and skeptics alike a lens to view the world that is both ancient and remarkably apt for the challenges of modernity. The Church affirms that the truth found in Christ is not confined to the sacred, but resonates in every facet of existence, from the mysteries of the universe to the deepest questions of human morality and purpose.

To articulate these ideas effectively, this book endeavors to bridge the diverse streams of Catholic teaching and apologetic practice. Through a structured exploration, it presents Catholicism as both a doctrinal journey and a lived experience. Topics span from foundational theological concepts like the dignity of the human person and the common good, to practical considerations such as Catholic social teaching's role in contemporary society. At its core, this book seeks to equip readers with the tools to explore, articulate, and defend their faith amid a world that so often misunderstands or even dismisses these eternal truths.

Through each chapter, readers will find an intricate system compiled of philosophy, theology, ethics, and history. This interweaving allows for a deeper appreciation of how Catholic doctrine shapes and is shaped by cultural and intellectual currents across centuries. The narrative invites scholars and thinkers from all walks—be they believers or seekers—to delve into an exploration of truth that extends beyond mere academic exercise into the very essence of life itself.

In essence, this introduction acts as both a map and a calling. It's a map that outlines the path through the rich landscape of Catholic thought, and a calling to embrace the journey with an open heart and analytical mind. By engaging with these enduring truths, we step into a conversation that transcends time—a dialogue between the divine and the human, the eternal and the temporal. It's a journey that promises not just to enlighten the mind but to enrich the soul.

Just as the Church emerges as a universal call to holiness, so too does this book echo that call. It invites readers into a thoughtful examination of Catholic doctrine as a living tradition, one that constantly renews itself by pursuing ever greater understanding and fidelity to the teachings of Christ. For the skeptic, the challenge is to engage deeply and openly; for the believer, it is to deepen one's own understanding and witness within a dynamic and often challenging world arena.

As we prepare to delve deeper into the heart of Catholic teaching, let us center our thoughts on the words of Jesus Christ, who has called us to love God with all our heart, soul, and mind. This pursuit of knowledge and faith is not merely an intellectual exercise, but a journey towards a greater love that seeks the good, the true, and the beautiful. As this exploration unfolds, may readers find themselves drawn into a fuller understanding of God's immense love and His plan for humanity.

This book is crafted as a guide—not merely to answer questions, but to encourage new ones. Through this dynamic engagement, we seek to foster a Catholic apologetic approach grounded in humility, charity, and clarity. As the reader progresses, each chapter builds upon the last, offering new vistas for understanding one's own position within the broad landscape of human belief and unbelief. The conversation started here aims to be both challenging and enriching, providing a firm foundation while encouraging profound personal and communal transformation.

So, with minds open to understanding and hearts open to belief, let us embark on this journey, considering each page a step towards deeper insight into the mystery of faith. We aim to see Catholicism not just as a last bastion of ancient belief, but as a living, breathing testament to the enduring relevance and transformative power of Christ's message in the world today.

Chapter 1: Overview of Catholic Social Teaching

Catholic Social Teaching (CST) serves as a rich composition of moral and ethical guidelines, rooted deeply in the Church's understanding of divine revelation and human purpose. At its heart lies an unwavering commitment to human dignity, seamless integration of faith and reason, and a call to love one's neighbor as oneself. This doctrine invites scholars, theologians, and skeptics alike to explore the depth and breadth of its teachings, which are grounded in the Gospel and have evolved through centuries of theological reflection and pastoral practice. A clear articulation of CST emphasizes its enduring relevance amidst contemporary social challenges, urging the global community towards justice, peace, and the common good. In this chapter, we set the stage for a comprehensive exploration of Catholic teachings, examining their foundations and historical progression as a beacon of hope and a catalyst for transformative action in the world. Through this lens, CST not only beckons to those within the Catholic faith but also extends its principles universally, proposing a vision of society where every human being can flourish in peace and dignity.

Foundations of Catholic Social Teaching

The fabric of Catholic Social Teaching (CST) is woven intricately with threads of both timeless truths and contemporary realities. Central to its foundation is the ancient wisdom derived from scripture and the teachings of Church Fathers. At its core, CST arises from the belief in the inherent dignity of the human person—a belief grounded in the notion that each person is created in the image and likeness of God. It's a call to recognize, uphold, and celebrate this dignity in every aspect of life, from the quiet corners of family life to the bustling dynamics of global politics.

The Incarnation, where God became flesh, elevates the status of humanity and underscores the Church's call to justice. This incarnational principle demands that Catholics see the face of Christ in every individual, compelling action towards the realization of justice and love. With this foundation, CST doesn't stand as a mere set of abstract principles but as a living guide compelling believers to act. It's a blueprint not only for personal sanctity but also for societal transformation.

Beyond its spiritual underpinnings, CST is deeply philosophical. It resonates with natural law traditions that advocate for universal truths discernible by reason. These truths are not arbitrary but are understood to be written in the hearts of all people, consistent globally and eternally. This universality of natural law calls Catholics to a moral responsibility beyond cultural and national confines, urging an active participation in the promotion of the common good.

Embedded within CST is the notion of solidarity—a commitment to the good of all, particularly those who are impoverished or marginalized. It's a call to move beyond mere compassion into concrete action, challenging believers to not only feel for others but to act with them. This sense of unity transcends personal and nationalistic boundaries, reminding Catholics of their shared humanity with all people regardless of their status or situation.

Intricately linked to solidarity is the principle of subsidiarity, which advocates that matters should be handled by the smallest, lowest, or least centralized competent authority. However, it recognizes the necessity of support from higher orders when local efforts are inadequate. The balance between these principles illustrates a profound respect for both personal initiative and communal responsibility, providing a framework for building societies that nurture human dignity and community well-being.

Catholic Social Teaching finds its voice not only in encyclicals and papal exhortations but also in the lived experiences of the faithful. Over centuries, it has responded to the cries of the poor and the demands of justice, articulating a vision that is ever ancient and ever new. Inspired by figures like St. Augustine and St. Thomas Aquinas, CST draws from a deep well of theological insight, offering a rich confluence of thought that is as relevant today as it was in centuries past.

The impact of CST goes beyond the Church's walls, influencing global conversations on issues like economic justice, human rights, and environmental stewardship. Its foundational principles offer a critical lens through which to evaluate contemporary social structures and policies, ensuring that the promotion of human dignity remains at the forefront.

In engaging with the world, CST models a distinctly Catholic way of living—one marked by a commitment to love and serve without distinction. It proposes a path that challenges both individuals and communities to conversion, urging a deeper alignment of personal and public life with the gospel message. Indeed, CST calls on Catholics to become artisans of a renewed humanity, co-workers in building God's kingdom on Earth.

The call to justice found in CST is not a burden but a path to liberation. It's a radical invitation to see and treat others as Christ himself, fostering communities where each person can flourish. As an embodiment of the Church's prophetic witness, CST confronts injustices with the audacity of hope, grounded in the theological trust that God's love will triumph over all manner of social evils.

Ultimately, the foundation of Catholic Social Teaching invites not just reflection but transformation. It's a call resonating from the Church's heart, whispering to the world what's possible when love and justice kiss. As Catholics engage with CST, they are prompted to become voices for the voiceless, hands for the helpless, and lights in the darkness. By living these teachings, they participate in a divine drama, where human frailty meets heavenly grace, crafting a future imbued with the possibility of redemption and renewal.

Thus, Catholic Social Teaching stands as a testament to the Church's enduring mission—the quest for a world reflective of God's kingdom, where peace and justice shall reign. It beckons believers to a deeper imitation of Christ, affirming that in serving others, they encounter the richness of God's presence amidst the complexities of the modern world.

Historical Development of Catholic Social Teaching

Catholic Social Teaching (CST) has a rich historical development that emerges from deep theological roots intertwined with the lived experiences of Christians throughout the ages. This body of thought is not static; rather, it evolves as society faces new challenges and opportunities. Its development traces back to biblical foundations, was given shape through the writings of Church Fathers, and reached formal expression in modern papal encyclicals.

The seeds of Catholic Social Teaching find soil in the Holy Scriptures, where the teachings of Jesus Christ provided profound insights into a society built on love and justice. The Old Testament spoke of God's covenantal love and justice, themes further elaborated in the New Testament, where Christ's mission was about healing society through love, compassion, and respect for each person's dignity. This biblical substrate is foundational, setting a stage for the Church's reflection on social issues across centuries.

In the early Church, the Church Fathers began to articulate social principles reflecting this scriptural heritage. Figures like Augustine and Basil the Great emphasized caring for the poor and the communal nature of human life. Augustine, in particular, designed a theological framework for society that rested on divine justice and charity. His works propose that societal peace is aligned with the divine, where both justice and love play integral roles. However, much of this remained theological musings until the Church faced social upheavals that required more concrete interventions.

Moving through the Middle Ages, the Church often found herself at the center of societal transformation. The economic and social theories of Thomas Aquinas offered further clarity. His synthesis of Aristotelian philosophy with Christian theology provided a robust framework for understanding the moral implications of economic and social interactions. Through his writings on the common good and justice, Aquinas laid the groundwork for later developments in modern Catholic Social Teaching.

Fast forward to the Industrial Revolution, where the world witnessed seismic shifts in technology, economy, and society. These changes brought about significant social injustices, from poor working conditions to widespread poverty. It was in this context that Catholic Social Teaching began to take its modern form. Pope Leo XIII's encyclical, *Rerum Novarum* (1891), marked a monumental turning point. This document addressed the rights and duties of capital and labor, setting a new path for the Church's engagement with modern social issues.

Rerum Novarum wasn't merely a response to immediate concerns but a foundational text that underpinned a century of CST development. It affirmed the dignity of workers, endorsed the right to private property while criticizing economic exploitation, and advocated for the role of the state in ensuring social justice. Its emphasis on the importance of community and the preference for the marginalized echoed doctrines that have long resounded in Christian tradition.

The social encyclicals that followed continued to build upon and expand the principles laid out by *Rerum Novarum*. Pope Pius XI's *Quadragesimo Anno* (1931) and Pope John XXIII's *Mater et Magistra* (1961) further articulated the Church's approach to evolving socio-economic landscapes, introducing concepts like subsidiarity and stressing the importance of social equity and human rights.

The Second Vatican Council also injected new vitality into Catholic social thought, broadening its global perspective. Documents such as *Gaudium et Spes* emphasized the role of the Church in the modern world, advocating dialogue and cooperation among all people for the common good. This broadened the scope of CST to include peace, disarmament, and issues related to international development.

Pope Paul VI and his successors have continued this trajectory. Encyclicals like *Populorum Progressio* and *Sollicitudo Rei Socialis* underscored the Church's commitment to global justice, lifting the voices of the developing world and emphasizing the interconnectedness of humanity. These documents widened the lens through which CST viewed issues, considering them within global socio-political and economic frameworks.

At the turn of the millennium, Pope John Paul II, with his encyclicals *Laborem Exercens*, *Centesimus Annus*, and *Evangelium Vitae*, continued to advance CST. His writings highlighted the dignity of human work, critiquing consumer culture, and addressed life issues with vigorous condemnation of practices that disregard life's sanctity. Furthermore, he encouraged a 'culture of life' as opposed to a 'culture of death,' articulating a vision that sees the person at the heart of social structures.

Pope Benedict XVI and Pope Francis have carried these themes into the 21st century. Pope Benedict's *Caritas in Veritate* broadened the discussion on the integral development of humans, while Pope Francis's *Laudato Si'* offered a compelling call for environmental stewardship within the context of CST, addressing the ecological crisis as an urgent moral imperative.

The historical development of Catholic Social Teaching reveals an enduring commitment to integrating faith and reason in the service of humanity. It is a teaching born out of lived experience, responding to the changing circumstances of history with timeless truths. This ever-evolving tradition continues to challenge and inspire the faithful as they navigate the complexities of modern existence in light of their call to love and promote justice. The journey of CST reflects a continuous dialogue between the Church and the world, embodying a vision of hope grounded in the Gospel of Jesus Christ.

Chapter 2: The Dignity of the Human Person

The dignity of the human person lies at the heart of Catholic social teaching, a cornerstone that both anchors and elevates our understanding of the human condition in relation to the divine. Rooted in the belief that every person is made in the image and likeness of God, this principle asserts that each individual's worth is not contingent upon societal status, achievements, or any external measure of success. It's a profound acknowledgment of an inherent value that transcends temporal realms, beckoning a respect for life and liberty that forms the bedrock of ethical engagement. This dignity calls us to act not out of mere obligation but a transformative love that seeks justice and mercy, embracing the marginalized and advocating for the voiceless. With such a perspective, human interactions are not reduced to transactions but seen as opportunities to manifest God's love and wisdom in the pursuit of a just social order. In this framework, the dignity of the human person becomes an unyielding lens through which we interpret and address the myriad complexities of modern life, challenging us to reflect on our own behaviors and the societal structures within which we operate.

Theological Basis for Human Dignity

In the grand tradition of Catholic theology, the concept of human dignity emerges as a vital component appearing in its very essence. It is a doctrine illuminating the conviction that every human life, regardless of circumstances, possesses a divine worth. This belief is not merely a product of philosophical musings but a reflection of foundational truths deeply rooted in the nature of God and His creation.

A central tenet of Catholic theology is the imago Dei, or the idea that human beings are created in the image and likeness of God. This is not a superficial resemblance but an ontological truth that forms the very core of human identity. In Genesis, the divine proclamation, "Let us make man in our image, according to our likeness," underscores the profound truth that human dignity is not an earned status but an inherent one.

The imago Dei bestows upon humanity an intrinsic dignity that does not fluctuate with societal status, ability, or merit. This dignity is not a societal construct but a divine ontological reality. It manifests in the unique capabilities of reason, free will, and the capacity for communion with God. Such capacities distinguish human beings from the rest of creation, affirming their exalted place in the order of things.

Saint Augustine, in his profound theological reflections, emphasizes the restlessness of the human heart until it finds rest in God. This metaphysical longing reflects the capacity for communion, a key aspect of human dignity. It is this very yearning that distinguishes the human spirit, elevating it above the mere material and aligning it with the divine.

Moreover, the Incarnation further amplifies the divine worth assigned to human beings. The Word made flesh in Jesus Christ signifies God's ultimate affirmation of humanity's dignity. By assuming human nature, Jesus sanctifies it, imbuing it with a dignity that transcends even the loftiest human aspirations. This divine condescension is both a testament to humanity's worth and a call to recognize and honor that dignity in every person.

The Church Fathers, ever zealous in their defense of human dignity, taught that Christ did not merely redeem humanity as a collective but as individuals, each possessing unique value. The Incarnation is a vivid reminder of the personal nature of God's love and the dignity inherent in being called by name. This individual call underscores the vastness of human worth, transcending any societal markers or limitations.

In exploring human dignity theologically, one cannot overlook the concept of freedom. Freedom, in the Catholic understanding, is not mere autonomy but the gift of self-determination aligned with truth and goodness. It is within this framework that true dignity is actualized. According to Saint Thomas Aquinas, freedom properly understood is the basis upon which humans choose to pursue the good and to forge authentic relationships with God and neighbor.

Aquinas further elaborates on the role of reason, emphasizing that it is through rationality and reason that humans participate in God's divine wisdom. This participation elevates the human intellect, endowing it with a dignity that calls one towards truth. Therefore, reason is not only a function but a reflection of the divine order, instilling humans with a unique value.

Another layer to consider in this discussion is the communal dimension of human dignity. Catholic theology posits that humans, while individually dignified, are also part of a larger body—the human family. This communal aspect is reflected in the mystery of the Trinity, where relationality and love are central. Therefore, dignity is both personal and collective, calling individuals to recognize and affirm the dignity of others.

In examining the passion and resurrection of Christ, we find the ultimate demonstration of human dignity's worth. The passion, with its radical sacrifice, underscores a love that elevates and redeems. The resurrection affirms not only victory over death but also the eternal value placed upon the human person. This does not merely restore humanity to its original state but elevates it to new heights of dignity.

Scripture and tradition consistently affirm that human dignity is a gift from God, sustained by His love and grace. The sacraments, as channels of divine grace, further affirm this dignity by incorporating individuals into the body of Christ. Each sacrament reinforces the truth that every individual is a cherished member of God's family.

The theological understanding of human dignity is not without its ethical imperatives. Recognizing the divine image within each person demands a corresponding action, a call to justice and love. It compels one to advocate for those marginalized and to ensure that every human life is treated with respect and care.

Thus, the implications of human dignity permeate every aspect of Catholic teaching and practice. It directs believers towards a vision of the world where every life is valued and every person is seen as a reflection of the divine. In this light, Catholic social teaching becomes not merely a set of guidelines but a profound commitment to embodying the gospel's transformative power.

As Catholic scholars and theologians, it becomes imperative to articulate and defend this theological basis in an increasingly secular world. It is a truth that speaks to the heart of human identity and purpose, challenging all to see beyond the temporal and embrace the eternal dignity bestowed by a loving Creator.

Ethical Implications of Human Dignity

The concept of human dignity, intrinsic to the human person, forms the cornerstone of Catholic social teaching and ethical thought. This foundational belief asserts that every human being, regardless of circumstance, holds an inherent value that is not earned through actions, talents, or social status. From the moment of conception, each person is imbued with this dignity, a precious gift from God that underscores the moral compass driving human interaction and societal structures.

The implications of this belief are vast and profound. Recognizing the innate dignity of every human being calls for a radical reevaluation of how society treats its members, especially those who are marginalized or vulnerable. It demands a shift from utilitarian perspectives, where individuals might be valued based on what they can contribute to society, to a viewpoint that honors each person's sacred worth. This is not merely a philosophical stance but a guide to living a life that respects the core of our shared humanity.

Ethically, embracing the dignity of the human person requires us to act and decide within a moral framework that sees all life as sacred. This vision challenges various societal norms that often evaluate worth based on productivity, appearance, or economic utility. It invites questions about how we approach issues like poverty, healthcare, and justice, urging us to develop systems and practices that enhance rather than diminish the value of human life. In every action and decision, individuals are called to reflect on how these align with the fundamental respect for human dignity.

Consider the implications for the healthcare system. If every patient's dignity is respected, then healthcare becomes not a commodity for the few but a basic human right. The ethical demand is that medical treatment prioritizes the wellbeing of the person, not the profitability of the system. Decisions regarding the allocation of scarce resources, like organ transplants or emergency care, must be navigated with a focus on proverbial justice and impartiality, ensuring that no life is deemed less worthy than another.

In addition, the workplace becomes a setting where respect for human dignity transforms power dynamics and community ethos. Workers are not mere cogs in a machine but persons deserving respect, fair wages, and humane working conditions. This shifts the discourse from economic gain for the employer to a cooperative engagement where dignity informs labor laws, corporate ethics, and interpersonal relationships.

Education, too, is reshaped under this paradigm. Schools and universities must recognize their role in teaching students about their inherent worth and the worth of others. Educational frameworks that emphasize character and ethics play a pivotal role in forming individuals who respect their own dignity and that of their peers. By fostering environments that cultivate respect, empathy, and understanding, educational institutions contribute to a society that mirrors these values.

Marriage and family life shine brightly when viewed through the lens of human dignity. Marriage becomes a partnership of equals, rooted in mutual respect and love. Family life is the soil in which dignity is first nurtured, encouraging compassion, responsibility, and moral fortitude. The faith community is tasked with supporting families in their mission to uphold and transmit these values, transforming society one family at a time.

This understanding of human dignity has profound policy implications, particularly in how societies address issues of inequality and injustice. Public policies must reflect the commitment to human dignity, driving initiatives that combat discrimination, poverty, and exploitation. Political leaders, inspired by this ethical framework, are called to craft legislation that upholds the dignity of all citizens, paying special attention to those on the margins.

Furthermore, the Church's moral teaching on bioethics is deeply informed by the principle of human dignity. Issues such as euthanasia, abortion, and genetic manipulation challenge us to consider the implications of technological advancements on our understanding of life's sanctity. Each bioethical dilemma should be approached with the recognition of God's imprint on every person, ensuring that scientific progress honors rather than overrides human dignity.

Global concerns, such as human trafficking and modern slavery, remind us of the dark areas where human dignity is still severely compromised. The call to recognize the dignity in every person urges us to actively engage in combatting these atrocities. Diplomacy, advocacy, and social action become tools through which the Church can demonstrate the depth of its commitment to the fundamental worth of each person.

The Catholic understanding of human dignity also has profound ecumenical and interfaith implications. Recognizing the dignity inherent in every person, regardless of religious background, provides a powerful common ground for dialogue and collaboration. As the Church engages with other faith communities, this shared understanding can foster peace, alleviate prejudices, and build bridges in a fractured world.

In conclusion, the ethical implications of human dignity as perceived in Catholic theology are not limited to personal morality but extend to the very fabric of societal structure. They challenge us to see beyond individual gain, inviting a collective journey toward a community that reflects the light of divine love and grace. Living with a deep awareness of human dignity calls for courage and commitment, but it is a call that promises the fruits of a more just, loving, and humane world. In every interaction, decision, and policy, may the dignity of each human person be the guiding light, a testament to our shared divinity and destiny.

Chapter 3: The Common Good

As we delve into the intricate nature of the common good, we uncover a fundamental principle that underpins the fabric of society, revealing itself as a guiding beacon for communal life. At its core, the common good refers not to the mere aggregation of individual interests but to the holistic flourishing of all individuals within a community. In the Catholic tradition, it is seen not only as a social obligation but as a divine directive, echoing the call to love one's neighbor as a reflection of God's love for humanity. This principle challenges us to consider the interconnectedness of humanity, prompting actions and policies that transcend personal gain, thus fostering environments where every person can achieve their potential. By prioritizing the common good, societies move closer to reflecting the kingdom of God on Earth, where justice, peace, and mutual respect reign supreme. It urges us to look beyond our own perspectives, to use our freedoms responsibly, and to engage in the civic life of our communities with genuine concern for all. Ultimately, the pursuit of the common good becomes an exercise in love, a testament to shared humanity, and a profound expression of our faith in a just and loving Creator.

Defining the Common Good

In the rich history of Catholic thought, the concept of the common good emerges as both a guiding principle and a moral beacon. Emerging from the depths of Catholic Social Teaching, the common good speaks to a universal call to action, beckoning individuals and societies towards a more just, equitable, and harmonious existence.

But what exactly is the common good, and how is it defined within Catholic theology? Simply put, the common good can be understood as the sum total of social conditions which allow people, either as groups or as individuals, to reach their fulfillment more fully and more easily. It encompasses the idea that the well-being of individuals is inseparably linked to the well-being of the community. The notion rejects individualism and utilitarianism, advocating instead a harmonious balance between personal freedom and communal responsibility.

Historically, the concept traces its roots back not only to the ancient philosophies of Aristotle and Plato but has been significantly developed by the Church Fathers and later thinkers. In their exploration, these philosophers and theologians concluded that the common good must acknowledge the complex interdependence that exists among all human beings.

The common good is not confined to a particular era or culture; it finds relevance throughout history as an essential aspect of moral philosophy. Its implementation demands ongoing discernment and application as societies evolve. For the early Christians, sharing resources and providing for the needy were natural expressions of this principle. In their communal life, they mirrored the Divine will, which seeks the flourishing of all creation.

Access to the common good, according to Catholic teaching, is a fundamental right. Every individual should have the opportunity to participate in social and economic life. This does not merely mean access to material goods but also includes other intangibles like peace, social justice, and cultural enrichment. The Church emphasizes that the needs of the poor and the marginalized often serve as a litmus test for the integrity of any claim to promote the common good.

Yet, it's important to recognize that the pursuit of the common good sometimes requires individuals and groups to forego certain liberties or personal gains. St. Thomas Aquinas taught that the common good requires the participation of all and that it is realized when every member of the community contributes to and benefits from it. Sacrifices made in the name of the common good are indeed reflections of selflessness and charity, virtues that lie at the heart of Christian ethics.

The notion also extends beyond mere human interaction, encompassing the stewardship of God's creation. In this light, the environment is not an object of possession but a sanctuary to be shared responsibly. Thus, the common good includes the careful and equitable management of resources, ensuring that future generations will equally enjoy and sustain them.

A key component of the common good is its relational aspect. Pope John XXIII noted that the common good must accommodate partisan interests with those of the broader community, indicating a continuous dialogue between personal interests and collective well-being. This relational aspect challenges individuals to venture beyond their immediate circles and consider their obligations towards broader humanity.

Catholic theologians have frequently highlighted that the pursuit of the common good is inherently linked to the principle of subsidiarity. While subsidiarity advocates for decision-making at the most local level possible, it safeguards the role of larger institutions in promoting the common good. In this relationship, the principle ensures that no community member is left behind, while local engagement permits tailored solutions and personal involvement.

Recognizing the challenge posed by globalization, the Church calls upon believers to widen the scope of their understanding of the common good. The interconnectedness of today's world stresses the need for international cooperation and collective responsibility. The common good extends boundaries, entering the realm of global solidarity, linking diverse peoples and nations in a shared destiny.

In contemporary society, articulating the common good requires addressing complex considerations concerning justice, peace, and the environment. Pope Francis, in his encyclicals, has emphasized the interconnectedness of these issues, urging a shift in perspective towards integrally addressing problems using a common good framework as a point of reference.

Furthermore, it's critical to acknowledge that the common good can't merely be imposed from above; it necessitates the participation of all levels of society. Regardless of differing capabilities, each person's active involvement is necessary for the vision of a collective well-being to materialize. The rich tapestry of individual contributions weaves a more robust societal fabric.

The philosophical underpinning of the common good is not solely an intellectual exercise but a call to action. It implores not only reflection but also commitment to enact its principles. Such real-world applications can be seen in how societies organize themselves economically, politically, and culturally, always seeking justice, equity, and peace.

Ultimately, the endeavor to define and implement the common good within the Catholic framework is a continual, evolving process. Rooted in love for the neighbor and reverence for God, the common good challenges the Church and each believer to reflect divine justice and mercy in the temporal world. It is a testament to Catholicism's profound commitment to the flourishing of humanity in light of divine will, urging every soul towards a responsible embrace of communal life. In so doing, it articulates an ideal towards which societies can strive, a beacon directing us towards a world reflective of God's original design for creation.

Role of the Common Good in Society

The concept of the common good is deeply embedded within Catholic social teaching, acting as a compass that guides societal actions towards justice and fraternity. This theme, woven intricately throughout the Church's history, calls us to look beyond individual interests and consider a broader vision that serves humanity at large. At its heart, the common good seeks to promote conditions that enable every person to flourish both individually and collectively. It challenges us to not only acknowledge but embrace, the interconnectedness of our lives, recognizing that each decision we make reverberates throughout the web of our shared existence.

In society, the role of the common good can be likened to the soul of a community, infusing intention and purpose into our collective endeavors. It's not merely an abstract principle but a living reality that manifests in various aspects of societal life. Consider, for a moment, how laws are instituted. In just laws, we find a reflection of the common good, as they aim to protect the rights and dignity of every person, fostering an environment where all can thrive. This is evident in the Church's teachings, where there is a constant emphasis on the alignment of human-made laws with divine justice.

A vital component of the common good is the principle of equality, urging society to address disparities and ensure that resources and opportunities are distributed fairly. It's a call to action for governments, institutions, and individuals alike to work towards dismantling structures that perpetuate inequality. The common good demands that our economic systems prioritize human dignity over profit margins, advocating for a model where wealth acts not as a tool for dominance but as a means to uplift and empower the marginalized.

Nevertheless, achieving the common good in society isn't without its complexities. It requires us to navigate the tension between personal freedom and social responsibility. A society oriented towards the common good recognizes that true liberty isn't found in self-centered autonomy but in a freedom oriented towards truth and goodness. This understanding calls us to sacrifice some personal aspirations for the sake of communal benefit. It's a paradox of our existence; true fulfillment often arises from embracing the needs of others.

Education plays a pivotal role in cultivating an understanding of the common good. From a young age, individuals can be taught to move beyond self-centered viewpoints and appreciate their contributions to the world. Catholic education, in particular, emphasizes this aspect by integrating principles of charity, justice, and social awareness. As individuals are molded with a consciousness that seeks the common good, they become equipped to enact positive change within their communities.

Let's turn our attention to technology and its rapid expansion, which presents both a challenge and an opportunity for the common good. On one hand, technological advancements can perpetuate isolation and detachment from the human experience; on the other, they can bridge gaps, offering innovative solutions to social issues. It falls upon society to harness technology in ways that enhance the common good, ensuring that its use amplifies our capacity for connection and understanding rather than division.

Furthermore, the Church calls us to look at environmental stewardship through the lens of the common good. Care for creation is a testament to our respect for God's handiwork. By acting as stewards of the earth, society safeguards the resources needed for future generations, strengthening our bond with all of creation. Ensuring the health of our planet isn't just an ecological necessity but a moral obligation, reflecting our commitment to the broader community of life.

Dialogue is another crucial element in the pursuit of the common good. Engaging with one another in honest and constructive conversation breaks down barriers and fosters a sense of unity. The common good thrives in environments where open communication is nurtured, drawing diverse perspectives together in a harmonious exchange aimed at greater understanding and cooperation. In a polarized world, this dialogue serves as a catalyst for peace and reconciliation.

The family unit often acts as a microcosm of the common good within society. By fostering love, support, and mutual respect, families provide the foundational experiences of community life. In the Catholic tradition, the family is revered as the "domestic church," a sanctum where the values of the common good are first learned and lived out. By nurturing families, society plants seeds of compassion and justice that grow to impact broader communities.

Lastly, the Church herself plays an instrumental role in promoting the common good. Through her teachings, sacraments, and actions, the Church offers a vision for society rooted in love and justice. She stands as a beacon of hope, advocating tirelessly for policies and actions that reflect the dignity of every human being. The Church's guidance helps shape a moral framework within which society can navigate the complexities of modern life with clarity and purpose.

As we reflect on the role of the common good in society, it becomes evident that this principle isn't just an ideal but a practical imperative. It beckons us to transcend personal ambitions for the sake of a shared prosperity. Within Catholic thought, the common good isn't merely a philosophical construct but a tangible pathway to the kingdom of God on earth. By committing to this principle, society moves towards a harmonious unity, where each individual's giftedness contributes to the flourishing of all.

In all its facets, the common good challenges us to reconsider the contours of our personal and collective aspirations, realigning them with a vision of society where justice, peace, and love prevail. Through this sacred journey, we are called not just to strive for a better world but to embody the divine impression of community, making visible the invisible threads that unite us all in brotherhood and sisterhood.

Chapter 4: Solidarity

Building upon the principles of Catholic Social Teaching, solidarity stands as a profound commitment that transcends mere empathy, urging believers to embrace a collective responsibility rooted in genuine love for neighbor. It is an active expression of the theological truth that all humanity shares a common destiny, designed by God, inevitably binding us to one another irrespective of personal differences or societal divides. In practice, solidarity calls us to fortify the bonds that bridge social chasms, nurturing a spirit of community and trust as we endeavor to alleviate suffering and injustice. This commitment is not optional but essential, leading us to recognize each person's inherent dignity as interconnected threads of a singular human quilt. Thus, the notion of "us" and "them" dissolves into a unified "we," a living testament to the body of Christ's inclusive and redemptive nature. In essence, solidarity invites Catholics and skeptics alike to journey beyond isolated existence into a meaningful communion that mirrors divine love, challenging each participant to become a beacon of hope in a fragmented world yearning for unity.

Understanding Solidarity

In a world often marked by division and fracture, the virtue of solidarity offers a counter-narrative: a vision of unity and communal support that transcends individual interests. At its core, solidarity is a steadfast commitment to the common good, a principle that lies at the heart of Catholic social teaching. But what exactly does it mean to understand solidarity from a Catholic perspective, and how does it manifest in both personal and collective dimensions?

Solidarity, as articulated by the Church, is not merely a feeling or vague sentiment of compassion. It's a firm and persevering determination to commit oneself to the common good because we are all responsible for all. The Church, through her social doctrine, perceives humanity as one family, where every individual is viewed as a brother or sister. This familial bond goes beyond cultural, ethnic, and national boundaries. It is informed by a theological understanding of humanity's shared destiny and collective journey toward fulfillment in God.

The philosophical underpinnings of solidarity can be traced back to the concept of the imago Dei, the belief that humans are created in the image and likeness of God. This belief establishes a fundamental equality and intrinsic value in every person. Due to this shared divine image, the well-being of each person is intricately tied to the well-being of others. Such a perspective challenges modern individualistic tendencies and calls for a vision of society where relationships are characterized by gratuitousness, justice, and peace.

Moreover, solidarity is grounded in Jesus Christ's own life and teachings. The incarnation itself—God becoming man—demonstrates a profound act of solidarity. Christ identified with the human condition, sharing our sufferings and joys. His ministry consistently illustrated solidarity, whether in comforting the outcast, healing the sick, or challenging unjust structures that marginalize the poor and weak. For Catholics, Christ remains the ultimate model of solidarity; His actions provide a template for how we are to engage with the world.

In exploring solidarity, it's essential to acknowledge the dynamic interplay between the individual and society. Each member of society is called to cultivate solidarity within personal relationships, yet there is also a communal dimension, recognizing that structures, institutions, and cultures must reinforce this virtue. Solidarity thus becomes a lens through which policies and societal norms are evaluated and critiqued, advocating for systems that promote human dignity and social justice.

Throughout history, numerous examples testify to the transformative power of solidarity. The life of Saint Teresa of Calcutta, who immersed herself in the plight of the poorest of the poor, reflects a life lived in profound solidarity. Her mission exemplifies how small acts of love, when rooted in solidarity, can challenge indifference and inspire change. Likewise, movements for civil rights and social justice, often animated by religious conviction, have anchored their efforts in the principles of solidarity, advocating for comprehensive societal reform.

Understanding solidarity also prompts reflection on the relationship between charity and justice. While charity involves direct acts of love and kindness towards others, solidarity calls for justice—the transformation of social structures that impede human flourishing. The two are complementary; acts of charity are enriched and sustained by a commitment to justice, while efforts for justice gain depth and authentic motivation through a spirit of charitable love.

In a world where poverty, inequality, and injustice remain rampant, understanding and practicing solidarity becomes an imperative. It is not just a lofty ideal but a mission entrusted to every Catholic—indeed, to every person of goodwill. As we navigate the complexities of the modern world, solidarity challenges us to embrace a radical interconnectedness that respects human dignity and prioritizes the wellbeing of all, especially the most vulnerable.

The task is not without challenges. In understanding and promoting solidarity, Catholics are called to engage in ongoing conversion, shedding attitudes that prioritize self-interest over community. It requires a shift from a mentality of scarcity and fear to one of abundance and generosity. Education and formation are crucial in this regard, empowering individuals and communities to discern and act in ways that embody and advance solidarity.

As we delve deeper into the understanding of solidarity, let us remember its profound capacity to foster genuine human development. It invites all to a shared responsibility, one that merges contemplation with action, individual integrity with collective initiative. Through solidarity, Catholics are not merely passive observers but active participants in crafting a more just and loving world, aligned with God's vision for His creation. In doing so, they not only fulfill their calling but also offer an invaluable witness to the world—a testament to the enduring relevance and transformative power of embracing solidarity in its fullest sense.

Practical Applications of Solidarity

In the system of Catholic social teaching, the thread of solidarity stitches together the fabric of human destiny. It is not simply an abstract principle, but a living, breathing tenet that finds its expression in the lived experiences of communities and individuals. The path of solidarity calls us to a greater communion with one another, urging a presence that transcends mere coexistence. This call is not isolated to the lofty halls of academia; it's a summons to action within the real world, where faith meets the pressing needs of daily life.

One can trace the footprints of solidarity in the Church's tradition, beginning with the early Christians in Acts, who held all things in common to support one another. This historical precedent sets a rich example, urging modern believers to look beyond their personal wealth and possessions. The true measure of adherence to solidarity lies in the willingness to share resources, recognizing that an abundance of goods and opportunities is not meant for individual flourishing alone but for the upliftment of all.

The parish community, too, becomes a crucible for honing the practice of solidarity. Here, shared worship serves as both the source and summit of togetherness. In celebrating the Eucharist, Catholics partake in a divine solidarity, a mystical union that fortifies the bonds among believers. This sacrament not only unites the faithful with Christ but also sends them forth to embody this unity in the world. Each parish initiative, whether feeding the homeless or supporting struggling families, becomes a manifestation of the call to solidarity.

In practical terms, solidarity should urge the Church's members to engage in acts of charity and justice. While charity addresses immediate needs, justice seeks systemic change. Catholic organizations often spearhead initiatives that blend both elements, advocating for policies that ensure fair treatment and equal opportunities for the marginalized. From fighting for just wages to advancing educational equality, these efforts echo the Biblical charge to love one's neighbor as oneself.

Solidarity also finds expression in the realm of ecumenical and interfaith dialogue. The Church acknowledges that despite theological differences, all people are created in God's image and thus deserve respect and cooperation. Building bridges with other faith traditions is a testament to solidarity that respects diverse beliefs while working towards shared goals. By focusing on common human concerns like poverty, climate change, and peace, Catholics can forge alliances that transcend confessional boundaries and demonstrate a testament to the unity of the human family.

The principle of subsidiarity, a companion in Catholic social teaching, guides the application of solidarity. It insists that decisions ought to be made at the most local level possible, allowing individuals and communities to have greater control over their lives. When applied correctly, subsidiarity ensures that the attempts to live out solidarity are contextually appropriate, empowering local communities to take the lead while receiving necessary support from larger entities.

In professional settings, solidarity transforms workplace dynamics. It encourages ethical business practices and fosters environments where employees are valued rather than exploited. Companies led by faithful principles of solidarity and subsidiarity often see better cooperation, job satisfaction, and productivity. These workplaces act as microcosms of Christian community, where the dignity of each worker is recognized and the fruits of labor are shared equitably.

Furthermore, the family unit represents the most immediate context where solidarity is practiced. Within the bounds of family life, individuals first learn the importance of mutual support and sacrifice. Parents model this principle by ensuring that the needs of children take precedence, illustrating that love is often expressed through self-giving. As families grow to embrace neighbors and communities, they become powerful agents for change rooted in the spirit of Christian unity.

Education, particularly Catholic education, also plays a critical role in the formation of solidarity-minded individuals. By instilling a sense of social responsibility and providing students with a global perspective, Catholic schools mold young hearts and minds that are conscious of their interconnectedness with others. Through service projects and social justice education, students are equipped to take initiatives that reflect their commitment to the common good.

Solidarity, as a guiding principle, calls for a personal commitment that often involves stepping outside of one's comfort zone. It challenges apathy and indifference, inviting believers to take an active stance against injustice and to work concretely towards a more just society. This requires a conversion of heart, where personal desires align with the mission of the Church to bring about the Kingdom of God on Earth.

In summation, the practical applications of solidarity are as varied as they are profound. They call for a radical reorientation of the self towards others and foster a culture of encounter and empathy. As the Church continues to champion this principle in its mission, it invites all its members to integrate this teaching into the texture of their daily lives. Solidarity, then, transforms from an abstract ideal into a powerful witness of the Gospel, living out the command to love and serve one's neighbor as oneself.

Chapter 5: Subsidiarity

Within the rich construct of Catholic social teaching, subsidiarity serves as a guiding beacon, emphasizing the importance of empowering smaller, local institutions to address issues in a manner responsive to their own unique contexts while acknowledging the role of higher authorities when necessary. This principle not only respects the dignity of each person but also fortifies the bonds of community, allowing for a harmonious balance where decisions are made at the most immediate level capable of resolving matters effectively. In essence, subsidiarity fosters both autonomy and unity, acknowledging the individual's potential while not losing sight of the collective good. Rooted in philosophical and theological foundations, it presents a compelling vision for societal organization that looks beyond mere efficiency to embody moral integrity and accountability. Thus, as we engage with this principle, we are invited to contemplate the rightful roles and responsibilities within the Church and society, ensuring that human dignity remains at the forefront of governance and interpersonal relations.

Concept of Subsidiarity

In Catholic social teaching, the concept of subsidiarity stands as a guiding principle designed to uphold human dignity and promote the common good. Rooted in both philosophy and theology, subsidiarity insists that matters ought to be handled by the smallest, lowest, or least centralized competent authority. As a functional principle, it not only preserves the autonomy of individuals and smaller communities but also demands accountability from larger institutions when smaller groups need assistance. This is a principle deeply anchored in the Church's understanding of human nature and society.

The idea of subsidiarity isn't new to the landscape of ethical and political thought. It draws from ancient philosophical traditions, which emphasize the importance of respecting individual and local capacities. In Catholic doctrine, subsidiarity first came to prominence in the encyclical *Quadragesimo Anno*, issued by Pope Pius XI in 1931. Here, subsidiarity was articulated as a response to the challenges of modern governance and industrialization. The Church saw the necessity to counterbalance the growing trend of centralization that threatened personal freedoms and local responsibilities.

At its core, subsidiarity operates on a foundation of trust and respect. It assumes that individuals and local communities have the inherent capacity to manage their own affairs and contribute to the welfare of society at large. Rather than stripping away the rights and responsibilities of smaller entities, subsidiarity seeks to empower them. When applied correctly, it provides an ethical framework that balances the scales between autonomy and intervention, ensuring that no level of society begins to encroach unreasonably upon the others.

Moreover, subsidiarity is not a call to isolation. It acknowledges the interconnectedness of all human society and recognizes that larger bodies, like governments or international organizations, have roles to play. However, these roles are largely supportive rather than directive, aimed at assisting without undermining the foundational efforts of smaller communities. The larger authority acts almost as an elder sibling, stepping in only when absolutely necessary and always with the intention of lifting the weaker or local authority back to a place of strength.

In practice, subsidiarity involves a dynamic interplay that demands discernment. It's not merely about the division of power; it's about fostering an environment where true human flourishing can occur. Decisions are ideally made closest to those who will be affected by them, ensuring that authority is not only distributed but also appropriately responsive to the needs and potential of the local level. This nuanced approach requires leaders who are both wise and humble, recognizing the limits of their own authority in pursuit of the broader common good.

Philosophically, subsidiary places great confidence in the capabilities of the human person. The Church teaches that each person is made in the image of God, endowed with reason and freedom, able to discern and choose the good. Consequently, subsidiarity encourages personal responsibility and creativity, pushing individuals to take ownership of their lives and problems, confident that they have the Church's support when burdened by challenges that exceed their capacity.

Theologically, the principle of subsidiarity echoes the relational nature of the Holy Trinity. Just as the Father, Son, and Holy Spirit engage in a mutual exchange of love and action, so too should human communities interact. Subsidiarity calls for a balance between unity and diversity, ensuring that larger institutions provide for the dignity and development of smaller ones without eclipsing their distinct roles and purposes.

In the context of Catholic social thought, subsidiarity cannot be viewed in isolation. It is intrinsically linked to other principles like solidarity and the common good. Together, these principles create a cohesive vision of how society should be structured, promoting justice, equity, and peace. Viewed holistically, subsidiarity informs our understanding of the social order and compels us to design systems protecting the inherent dignity of every person.

Consider how subsidiarity shapes our approach to economic systems. It challenges unbridled capitalism by warning against excessive centralization of economic power that diminishes human dignity. Similarly, it offers a critique of state-managed socialism by advocating for individual initiative and the rights of families and communities to make autonomous economic decisions. Subsidiarity, therefore, calls for a balanced economic policy that respects local endeavors while safeguarding against exploitation and injustice.

The implementation of subsidiarity demands a level of discernment and wisdom that is often challenging yet profoundly rewarding. It resonates with the moral responsibility of global leaders and citizens alike, demanding that everyone plays their part in fostering environments where the vulnerable are protected, and the strong empowered to serve justly. This principle asks Catholics to reflect on their roles within their families, workplaces, communities, and governments, urging a life that mirrors the ordered yet dynamic love found in the divine.

In conclusion, the concept of subsidiarity offers a compass guiding Catholic engagement with societal structures, ensuring that the dignity of the human person remains at the forefront of all social, economic, and political considerations. It's not merely an academic or theoretical construct but a living, breathing principle that informs our actions and decisions. Subsidiarity requires us to continually evaluate and reevaluate our structures, systems, and hierarchies, holding them accountable to the divine blueprint where justice, love, and peace are the true measures of progress.

Subsidiarity in Practice

The principle of subsidiarity, as integral as it is to Catholic social teaching, finds its true impact not merely in abstract discussions but in the tangible realities of everyday life. Like a stone cast into a pond, its ripples extend far beyond theoretical boundaries, enhancing the dignity and autonomy of individuals and communities alike. Its practical applications serve as a conduit connecting the Church's teachings with the complexities of a continually evolving world.

At its core, subsidiarity champions the idea that decisions should be made at the most immediate level of authority capable of addressing a matter effectively, yet without displacing the crucial roles of higher structures. Thus, it becomes imperative for individuals, families, and communities to assume an active role in their societal contributions. Rather than relying on distant or disconnected entities to dictate local governance or community aid, subsidiarity encourages local leadership and participation, energizing those at the grassroots level to engage actively with their circumstances.

Consider the family, often termed the domestic Church. It is here that subsidiarity first takes root. Within the family unit, parents are the primary educators of their children, imbued with the responsibility and authority to nurture their offspring in faith, morals, and education. Subsidiarity respects this natural order, suggesting that outside intervention from the state or larger institutions should only occur when the family cannot fulfill its duties. It advocates for empowering families with the resources and freedom to discharge their essential roles, which subsequently fosters the development of mature, responsible individuals capable of contributing positively to society.

Subsidiarity also finds expression in local governance. By entrusting communities with the authority to manage their local affairs, subsidiarity not only promotes efficiency but also spurs civic engagement. Local governments, parishes, and neighborhood organizations are better acquainted with the immediate needs and cultural nuances of their environments than are centralized authorities. They can tailor solutions with precision, resulting in outcomes that align with the common good.

Furthermore, the principle is evident in economic life. It rejects both collectivist approaches that strip away individual initiative and laissez-faire attitudes that ignore the common good. Instead, it advocates for an economic system where individuals and smaller entities, such as small businesses or cooperatives, are empowered to thrive. These smaller entities contribute to the economic system with innovation and personalized service that larger institutions might overlook. Subsidiarity underscores the importance of policies that support these entities, ensuring they are neither overwhelmed by burdensome regulations nor left to navigate an economy that favors massive corporations at their expense.

Subsidiarity in practice extends to the realm of education. Catholic schools exemplify this principle by fostering environments where students' unique gifts and potentials are recognized and nurtured. These educational institutions operate with an understanding of local culture and community needs, allowing them to tailor curricula and resource allocation effectively. Through subsidiarity, educational organizations gain the flexibility to address the particular needs of their students, generating a holistic and personalized learning experience that aligns with broader educational objectives.

One must not ignore the critical role the Church itself plays in realizing subsidiarity. The hierarchical nature of the Church is not a mechanism for controlling individual faith communities but rather a framework to guide and support them. Each parish community, while part of the larger Church, is encouraged to develop its ministries and outreach programs. This allows the faithful to address local needs in a manner coherent with the universal call to charity and evangelization. Such autonomy within unity ensures that the Church responds dynamically to the diverse challenges it faces worldwide.

However, applying subsidiarity is not without challenges. In contexts where resources are limited, smaller units may struggle to fulfill their roles adequately, necessitating external support. It becomes crucial to strike a balance where supplemental aid empowers rather than engenders dependency. Moreover, understanding the boundaries between intervention and autonomy can be nuanced, requiring discernment and a profound commitment to the common good.

In a globalized society, subsidiarity also informs international relations. Nations are called to cooperate in a manner that respects each other's sovereignty while addressing collective issues such as climate change, poverty, and migration. The Catholic Church advocates for international policies that empower nations to address their citizens' needs effectively, ensuring that assistance is both appropriate and respectful of local context.

Finally, subsidiarity fortifies the call to personal responsibility. By encouraging individuals to use their talents and abilities consciously, it fosters a culture of accountability and stewardship. Each person is recognized as an integral part of the larger human family, with a unique role to play in advancing justice, peace, and the common good.

In conclusion, subsidiarity in practice manifests as a vibrant principle that challenges and inspires us to rethink our roles within the intricate web of society. By championing the small and the local, it reminds us of the collective power inherent within individuals and communities. Far from being merely a guiding ideal, subsidiarity is a call to action that, when embraced, promises a more participatory, just, and compassionate world—a world where each human person can flourish in dignity, looking beyond oneself to weave bonds of solidarity and community.

Chapter 6: The Option for the Poor and Vulnerable

In weaving the fabric of society, the Catholic Church holds an unwavering focus on the preferential option for the poor and vulnerable, a principle deeply embedded in the Gospel's essence. This option isn't a mere suggestion but a fundamental axis around which moral reasoning orbits. It's based on the recognition that the divine image reflects equally and most vividly in those who suffer deprivation and marginalization. Theologically, Christ's own life and mission exemplify this commitment. He walked among the marginalized and the downtrodden, not as an observer, but as one who shares in their burdens and elevates their dignity. Thus, true Christian discipleship and evangelization endeavor to embody solidarity with the impoverished, urging action that transcends sentimentality to engage in social structures that perpetuate inequality. The Church, therefore, challenges us to eschew complacency and to embody an incarnational love that transforms society by advocating for just systems and offering tangible aid. This relentless advocacy acts as a testament to the Church's fidelity to Christ's teachings, affirming that our collective salvation is intrinsically linked to the well-being of the least among us.

Theological Insights on Poverty

The concept of poverty has long been a central focus in Christian theology, particularly within Roman Catholic teaching. Understanding poverty requires delving into a multifaceted issue that sees humanity entwined with both physical needs and spiritual conditions. Theologically speaking, poverty isn't merely an economic shortfall but a critical lens through which we engage with key tenets of faith such as compassion, love, and justice. The option for the poor underscores the church's mission to prioritize the needs of the less fortunate, reflecting the heart of Christ's ministry in the Gospels.

At its core, the preferential option for the poor is not just an agenda but a theological principle deeply embedded in the life and teachings of Jesus. Christ himself declared in the synagogue of Nazareth His mission to bring good news to the poor (Luke 4:18). This declaration sets the tone for a recurring theme throughout the Gospels, where the marginalized frequently find themselves at the center of divine favor. By prioritizing those in need, Christ reveals God's preference for those who suffer, calling the Church to echo this preference in its teachings and actions.

From a philosophical perspective, poverty can be understood as a negation of the natural human state as intended by God. The deprivation of basic needs—such as food, shelter, and dignity—contravenes the divine vision of human flourishing. The propagated sin of systemic injustice perpetuates poverty, making it not merely an individual moral failing but rather a structural issue requiring collective moral rectitude. In recognizing this, the Church's approach to poverty becomes not only about charity but about justice, seeking to dismantle the barriers that keep people oppressed.

St. Thomas Aquinas posits poverty as a condition that can potentially lead to greater spiritual insight and dependency on God, though it remains undesirable in its forced form brought about by societal failures. Voluntary poverty, as chosen by religious orders, contrasts with the involuntary poverty that the poor endure and highlights a profound spiritual insight—choosing poverty as an act of solidarity with the poor, and as a means to achieve a purer form of community with God.

Gaudium et Spes, one of the foremost documents of the Second Vatican Council, emphasizes that 'the joys and the hopes, the griefs and the anxieties of the men of this age, especially those who are poor or in any way afflicted, these are the joys and hopes, the griefs and anxieties of the followers of Christ.' Here, poverty forms a common ground for communal experience shared and uplifted within Christ's body, the Church, manifesting its solidarity with humanity overall but especially with those most in need.

The option for the poor also calls attention to a profound theological reality: the kingdom of God initiated through Christ is a kingdom of service, where power is measured by one's service to those on the fringes. Jesus flipped the societal hierarchies of His time, showing that true leadership exists in humble service to others. Examining the Beatitudes, one finds a roadmap of this inverted kingdom where the poor, the meek, and the persecuted are blessed, embodying the values of a radically inclusive love.

Given this theological vision, the Church's call to action encompasses both spiritual and temporal aspects. Spiritually, there is the necessary engagement with repentance, recognizing how personal and structural sins contribute to poverty. The Church calls her members to a genuine conversion of heart, where awareness of the poor is a spiritual discipline. Temporal action, however, cannot be overlooked, for it involves the concrete expression of love in advocacy and systemic change. The faithful are challenged to work towards economic and social systems that recognize the dignity and rights of every person.

Moreover, the Eucharistic celebration itself serves as a profound enacted theology of poverty. In the Eucharist, believers are reminded of Christ's self-emptying—His chosen poverty—to enrich humanity spiritually (2 Corinthians 8:9). Sharing in the Eucharist becomes an act of solidarity with the poor, inviting all members of the Christian community to live their lives in self-giving service, mirroring Christ's sacrificial love.

In conclusion, the theological insights on poverty articulated in Catholic teaching are rich with complexity and depth. They call believers to live in a manner that reflects divine love and justice. Through an unflinching preference for the poor, the Church commits to embodying the Gospel in its entirety, offering a life of hope and dignity to those on whom society has turned its back. This is not only a challenge but a divine invitation to partake in the transformative power of love made visible through action, fueled by faith and hope in God's unending goodness.

Strategies to Assist the Poor

In our discourse on "The Option for the Poor and Vulnerable," we've already explored its theological underpinnings. Now, we turn our attention to practical strategies designed to assist those who find themselves on the margins of society. This imperative, grounded in the Gospel message and the teachings of the Church, calls us to act with both charity and justice.

Recognizing the dignity of every human person, no matter their economic or social status, forms the bedrock of our approach. The Church envisions a world where resources are shared equitably, ensuring that all individuals can lead dignified lives. We are called to be the stewards who bring this vision to fruition. To start, one must consider systemic change, targeting the structures that perpetuate poverty and inequality.

Community Engagement and Empowerment

Community engagement is not merely an option but a necessity. When people work together in mutual support, they create a network that far surpasses individual efforts. The Church plays a pivotal role in fostering community development initiatives. By working with local leaders and community members, we can identify the needs specific to each locale and tailor solutions accordingly. This approach ensures that the unique circumstances and inherent capacities of each community are respected and leveraged.

Moreover, empowering communities involves educating and equipping individuals with the skills and knowledge necessary to improve their circumstances. Educational programs—ranging from basic literacy to vocational training—pave the way for self-sufficiency, allowing people to lift themselves out of poverty. The empowerment paradigm is about walking alongside those we serve, not imposing solutions from above.

Advocacy for Just Policies

While charity addresses immediate needs, justice demands systemic change. Advocacy for policies that protect the poor and vulnerable is essential. This involves engaging with policymakers to craft legislation that safeguards the rights and dignity of all, particularly those who cannot speak for themselves. As faithful stewards, we must push for reforms in areas like healthcare, housing, education, and employment to create a more just and equitable society.

In this mission, collaboration with other organizations that share a commitment to social justice amplifies our efforts. Working in coalitions can place pressure on decision-makers and illuminate the issues at hand. Such partnerships extend beyond interfaith collaborations; they include secular entities committed to promoting the common good.

The Role of Almsgiving and Direct Service

Almsgiving remains a fundamental Christian practice, reflecting our call to share our goods with those in need. While systemic change is critical, we must not overlook the immediate needs of individuals. Direct service—food pantries, shelters, and medical clinics—provides for the urgent necessities of the poor and must continue.

However, it's crucial that almsgiving and direct service meet not just the physical needs but also attend to the spiritual and emotional well-being of individuals. Offering companionship, listening to their stories, and treating each person with the dignity they deserve, represents the heart of our mission.

Beyond providing immediate relief, direct service initiatives offer opportunities for encounter and evangelization. These moments create spaces for building relationships, where the love of Christ can be both witnessed and expressed.

Transformative Education and Economic Opportunities

The creation of economic opportunities ranks among the most effective strategies for sustainable poverty alleviation. Education is a powerful tool in this regard. Religious and secular educational institutions must emphasize a curriculum that prepares students not only for employment but also for active participation in societal transformation.

Microfinance initiatives and cooperative businesses serve as practical means to empower individuals economically. By providing access to capital and markets, these initiatives allow people to realize their entrepreneurial potential. They act as catalysts for economic independence, breaking the cycle of poverty and enabling families to thrive.

Additionally, supporting fair trade practices ensures that products and services from the poor receive fair compensation. This aligns closely with the Church's teaching on the dignity of work and the rights of workers, emphasizing that economic systems should serve humanity, not the other way around.

Integration of Faith and Action

The Gospel calls us to integrate faith with action. As Catholics, our charitable endeavors and strategies to alleviate poverty should be deeply rooted in our faith's teachings. The liturgies, sacraments, and prayers of the Church provide sustenance and strength as we labor for justice.

Sacramental life, particularly the Eucharist, nourishes our commitment to social justice. In receiving Christ, we are commissioned to serve him in the least among us. Thus, our activism flows naturally from our liturgical life, embodying the Church's mission in the world.

The formation of this faith-action nexus can involve laying out the connections between Catholic teachings and daily life, helping individuals and communities alike see how their actions make God's love tangible.

In conclusion, assisting the poor involves a multifaceted approach grounded in the richness of Catholic social teaching. From empowering communities to advocating for justice, extending direct aid, fostering economic independence, and integrating faith with action, we are called to enact the love of Christ in a world yearning for transformation. This dimension of our faith challenges us to be both hearers and doers of the Word, living out the radical call to love and serve our neighbor.

Chapter 7: The Dignity of Work and Rights of Workers

In the sacred deposit of Catholic teaching, work emerges not merely as a necessity but as a sanctified act of human expression. This view is firmly rooted in the divine creation account where humanity is called upon to steward the earth, transforming labor into a noble act that carries inherent dignity. For Catholic thought, the right to work is inseparable from the dignity of the worker, entailing just wages, safe conditions, and the freedom to voice concerns without fear of reprisal. These principles assert that economic structures must serve the human family, not vice versa, underscoring a deep moral imperative: the advancement of justice in the workplace. As threads are woven to form fabric, so too do individual acts of labor weave a society that reflects the tenets of solidarity and respect, creating a seamless garment of the common good. In this harmonious vision, the rights of workers are not abstract ideals but vital tenets that echo the broader aspiration of the Church to uphold human dignity in every corner of society.

Theology of Work

Within the rich history of Catholic theology, the concept of work occupies a pivotal role, intertwining with the divine plan for human existence. The theology of work underscores not merely the practical and economic aspects of labor but illuminates its transcendental significance, as espoused by the Roman Catholic Church. It reminds us that work is more than a task; it is a calling, a vocation integrating human creativity with divine purpose.

In Genesis, we find the foundational narrative where God creates mankind in His image, endowing them with the mandate to "fill the earth and subdue it" (Genesis 1:28). The act of creation itself is presented as labor, a divine archetype that sanctifies human toil and elevates it beyond mere survival or economic necessity. This divine model affirms that work is intrinsically good, a reflection of God's own creative activity. Through work, humans participate in the continuous unfolding of creation, molding and transforming nature in service of God's kingdom.

Saint John Paul II, in his encyclical "Laborem Exercens," emphasizes that work is a fundamental dimension of human existence and not merely a means of fulfilling material needs. This perspective builds upon the enduring principle that work must serve the person's dignity, not the other way around. Work should enhance our humanity, not diminish it. It should respect the dignity of the person, for every occupation—be it menial or managerial—holds within it an opportunity for transformation and fulfillment.

The artistry of the Christian understanding of work is recognizing that it can become a means of sanctification. The mundane task, when approached with a spirit of dedication and love, becomes a conduit for divine grace. Yet, this perspective does not overlook the challenges and hardships often associated with labor. The toil and sweat of work are, in part, a reminder of the fall from grace, casting shadows of struggle upon human endeavors. Despite this, work remains a field where redemption can play out, where humanity can reconcile with creation and echo the redemptive act of Christ.

Moreover, the Catholic theology of work interweaves with the concept of community and the common good. Labor is not a solitary endeavor but a collaborative one, contributing to the well-being of others and the greater society. In this light, work evolves into a testament of solidarity, a testament that binds humanity together in common purpose. When we labor, we engage in a communal exchange, enriching ourselves and others, building the City of God amidst the city of man.

The notion of justice permeates the theology of work with demands for just wages and fair treatment, echoing the Church's mission to uphold human rights. Work environments must honor human dignity, reflecting the kingdom values of fairness and ethical integrity. Thus, questions of unemployment, exploitation, and economic disparity are not just social or economic issues; they become matters of theological concern. The Church stands as an advocate for those marginalized within the workplace, urging us to create systems that reflect the justice of God's kingdom.

Aquinas spoke to the importance of intention within the moral framework of human actions, and this extends to the sphere of work. The intention behind our labor transforms it, elevating it from mere action to a virtuous endeavor. Hence, work done with love becomes an expression of charity, aligning with the cardinal virtues. Such work has intrinsic worth, echoing the divine economy, where the measure of success is in faithfulness, not fortune.

The spirituality of work includes a Sabbatical principle as well, emphasizing the necessity of rest and reflection. This is not merely for rejuvenation of the physical but touches upon the deeper rhythm of work and repose reflective of our spiritual nature. The Sabbath commandment calls us to cease from labor and recognize God as the ultimate provider, reminding us of our dependence on Him and our need for spiritual nourishment.

Interconnected with this theology is an acknowledgment of the creative impulse within labor. Human work, in its essence, is an extension of God's creative act. This creativity is not limited by the boundaries of specific tasks but is instead present in the smallest of duties. Everything from crafting a fine piece of art to shaping legislation bears witness to the divine image within us, calling forth ingenuity and resourcefulness.

Furthermore, the theology of work invites a transformative vision of existing societal structures. It impels us to reimagine economies not solely as mechanisms of profit generation but as fields of just distribution and equitable opportunity. Catholic teaching envisions an economic order where profit serves the human person, not the other way around. This vision integrates economic productivity with ethical responsibility, aiming towards a society where work supports and uplifts human lives.

Ultimately, the theology of work calls us to recognize our roles as co-creators with God, entrusted with the stewardship of the earth and the shaping of our own destinies. It challenges us to find the sacred within the secular, imbuing every task with meaning and purpose that reflects God's loving design. By engaging in work with this understanding, we contribute to the miracle of God's creation, inserting our lives into the larger narrative of divine love and redemption.

Worker Rights in the Catholic Context

In the Catholic tradition, the rights of workers are not merely ancillary to economic and social theory but are embedded within the very core of human dignity and moral ethics. The Church, through her social teachings, presents work as more than a means to earn a living. It is a fundamental expression of human dignity, a way of participating in God's creation. Central to this understanding is the belief that labor is an intrinsic human act, one that is uniquely interwoven with the moral and spiritual fabric of the individual.

The theological basis for the rights of workers draws extensively from the essence of human dignity as illuminated by the Church. Humans, created in the image and likeness of God, are granted a unique position in the order of creation, and it is within this framework that work is considered a sacred activity. The Catholic Church further argues that every laborer has an inherent right to conditions that protect their dignity, including just wages, safe working environments, and the ability to form associations or unions.

Historically speaking, the Church has been a steadfast advocate for workers' rights, especially during epochs where industrialization imposed stark inequities in societies around the world. Since the landmark encyclical "Rerum Novarum" by Pope Leo XIII in 1891, the Church has consistently emphasized the importance of just labor practices, asserting that workers should not be treated as mere economic commodities. Here, the principle of justice is pivotal, dictating that a fair day's work deserves a fair day's pay.

Catholic teaching stipulates the necessity for all work to be treated with respect and for workers to be provided with opportunities for personal and communal development. This aligns closely with what the Church calls the "universal destination of goods" — an ethical principle advocating that the fruits of the world's labor should ultimately benefit all, not just a privileged few. Work, then, is seen not as an isolating chore, but as a collaborative activity aiding in the advancement of the community and the common good.

An examination of the rights bestowed upon workers within the Catholic context reveals a profound concern with social justice. Justice, as a cardinal virtue, is a compass directing the ethical execution of labor relations. As enunciated in various Church doctrines, the rights to employment, participation, and basic economic security are essential. These rights stem not from an abstract moralism but from the lived realities of workers who deserve both protection against exploitation and avenues for personal and social flourishing.

The Church's focus on the dignity of work extends also to the right of workers to spiritual and physical rest. In this regard, the observance of Sunday as a day of rest is not simply a religious edict but an acknowledgment of the human need for rejuvenation and reflection. The Sabbath is a time to withdraw from labor, deepen one's relationship with God, and foster familial and communal bonds.

One must also consider the Church's discernment on the ethical implications of automation and technological advancements. As the nature of work evolves, Catholic social teaching encourages an ongoing discourse on ensuring that technology serves humanity rather than dehumanizing it. It's essential that technological progress does not create new forms of inequality or replace labor in ways that strip workers of their dignity and economic security.

Moreover, in defining the rights of workers, there is an intrinsic call to exercise solidarity. Solidarity implores individuals and institutions to stand together in mutual support, bridging divides, promoting unity, and advocating for the most vulnerable workers. This inherent duty underscores the essential bonds that weave society together, stressing the Church's vision of a world where labor relations mirror the values of compassion and justice.

The Church's perspective on labor rights often challenges prevailing economic systems, urging a re-evaluation of policies that solely prioritize profit over people. Such calls are rooted in the belief that economic and social systems must always serve the human person, not vice versa. This vision persists today, compelling advocate for economic structures that enable and support genuine human and community development.

Finally, the value that the Catholic Church places on the rights of workers inherently calls for vigilance and active participation in civic life. It invites both individuals and communities to engage with systems of power, prompting policy changes that reflect these deep-seated convictions around dignity and justice. By advocating for these rights, the Church provides a compass for ethical corporate and political actions.

In summary, the Catholic perspective on worker rights is an extension of an enduring commitment to uphold human dignity against the challenges of a changing world. This approach not only empowers individuals but also nurtures societies, providing a moral framework that guides the pursuit of a just, equitable, and compassionate world for all those engaged in the act of work.

Chapter 8: Care for God's Creation

In the embrace of divine love, the Catholic Church calls upon all of us to treat the Earth not merely as a resource but as a gift, a sacred trust bestowed upon humanity by the Creator. This stewardship demands that we acknowledge the interconnectedness of all life and the profound responsibility that this relationship entails. Rooted deeply in scripture and tradition, care for God's creation is an imperative that transcends mere environmentalism, positioning itself as a moral and spiritual duty. Just as God saw the fruits of creation and deemed them good, so too must we see our world with wonder and a commitment to preserving its beauty and integrity for future generations. By engaging in sustainable practices and advocating for the protection of our common home, we answer a higher calling—one that honors the divine artistry of creation and reflects our profound respect for the intricate web of existence that God has so lovingly woven. Through this lens of ecological transformation, we participate in the divine, becoming co-creators in nurturing the world to mirror the kingdom of heaven itself.

Environmental Stewardship

To delve into the subject of environmental stewardship within the framework of "Care for God's Creation" is to embark on a journey that touches the very essence of our existence. At its core, environmental stewardship encompasses the responsibility that humanity holds for the environment, a concept that finds deep roots in Catholic teachings. It's a call to nurture and protect the world, seeing it not merely as a resource to be exploited, but as a sacred gift entrusted to us by God. This responsibility is not an abstract idea; instead, it is a profound expression of our faith in action.

The principle of environmental stewardship emerges naturally from the belief that the world, in its entirety, is a divine creation—designed by the hands of the Almighty. A system so meticulously crafted that each element, whether it be the smallest microbe or the largest ecosystem, plays a vital role in the balance of life. It is here that we, as stewards, must act not as tyrants and despoilers but as the caretakers of this magnificent masterpiece. A testament to our role is vividly expressed in the Scriptures, where dominion over the earth is bestowed upon humankind. This dominion, however, is one of service and stewardship, requiring us to tend and care, as we would a garden.

When considering environmental stewardship in the Catholic context, it becomes evident that our approach is deeply philosophical and theological, not just ecological. This stewardship is seen as a moral imperative that beckons us to love all of God's creation with tenderness and respect. We are drawn to reflect on the concept of integral ecology, an idea championed by Pope Francis in his encyclical "Laudato Si': On Care for Our Common Home." This integral ecology emphasizes the interconnectedness of the environment, economy, and social justice, demanding a comprehensive approach that considers the totality of human experience.

Indeed, the theological underpinnings of environmental stewardship go beyond mere preservation. They direct us to the heart of Catholic social teaching, calling upon virtues such as prudence and justice. Prudence guides us in making wise decisions about the use and care of natural resources, ensuring that our actions serve the common good of present and future generations. Justice, on the other hand, requires us to recognize the rights of all creatures, and humankind's duty to uphold the dignity inherent within them.

Perhaps, one of the most intriguing facets of environmental stewardship is its capacity to unite disparate factions under a common cause. Regardless of political or ideological stances, the care for God's creation stands as a universal mandate that appeals to the innate morality within each person. It calls for a collective action attentive to both the cry of the earth and the cry of the poor, understanding that they are inextricably linked. The degradation of the environment often exacerbates poverty, hence why the Church advocates for solutions that are both environmentally and socially sustainable.

The implications of environmental stewardship extend into the realm of ethics, inviting each of us to deeply consider our lifestyle choices. Every decision, from what we consume, to how we dispose of waste, becomes an opportunity to express our commitment to God's creation. This conscious living, inspired by the Gospel values, is an embodiment of our relationship with God. It challenges individuals, communities, and nations to act responsibly, nurturing a sense of solidarity that transcends temporal boundaries.

It is in this challenge that we find a call to action. To implement practices that reflect our commitment to environmental stewardship involves a transformation in the way we perceive progress and success. Aligning development with sustainability requires humility and recognition of the limits of our knowledge and capabilities. It demands innovative approaches that are rooted in respect for the natural world, demonstrating that economic growth and environmental care are not mutually exclusive but are deeply intertwined.

In practice, Catholic communities worldwide have responded to the call for environmental stewardship through various initiatives. From parish-driven recycling programs to sustainable farming practices by Catholic organizations, the Church demonstrates its commitment to caring for God's creation. Educational efforts aimed at raising awareness about ecological issues also play a critical role, inspiring individuals to take proactive measures in their own lives.

Our journey in environmental stewardship is guided by a sense of profound reverence and awe for the beauty and complexity of God's creation. As we strive to fulfill our role as stewards, let us also be reminded of the hope and redemption offered by the faith. By aligning our actions with the divine will, we partake in the redemption of all creation and echo the grace of the Creator Himself. In this way, environmental stewardship becomes not only an ethical obligation but an act of worship, one that unites us with the transcendent purpose of our existence.

Practical Steps for Caring for Creation

In the intricate system of Catholic social teaching, caring for creation stands as a resounding call to duty—a duty inherent in the fabric of our faith and our relationship with God's world. Recognizing the Earth as a divine gift, we are entrusted with its stewardship, a charge that requires both reflection and action. Emphasizing the "why" and the "how" of environmental responsibility allows us to see the beauty in our collective mission.

First and foremost, understanding the theological context is essential. The Church's teachings remind us that creation is not merely a resource but a reflection of the Creator Himself. Our care for the environment is, therefore, an act of worship and gratitude. We are asked to see the world not as a possession but as a sacred trust. Indeed, our dominion over Earth calls us to a partnership with creation, emphasizing sustainability over exploitation.

Now, let's dive into the practical steps. The foremost approach involves fostering a renewed consciousness about how our daily choices impact the Earth. Simple adjustments in our lifestyle, from conserving water and energy to reducing waste, are steps everyone can take. By minimizing our ecological footprint, we begin to live in harmony with the planet we call home.

1. Educate and Advocate: Empowering oneself through education about environmental issues is crucial. Knowledge becomes the bedrock for informed action. Engage with Church resources that explore ecological concerns and Catholic teachings on environment stewardship. Through understanding, we can become advocates for sustainable practices within our communities. Speaking up for policies that protect the environment aligns our civic duties with our spiritual commitments.

2. Support Sustainable Practices: In our consumer habits, opting for sustainable products and supporting businesses that prioritize eco-friendly practices is key. The market's demand often shapes how businesses operate. By choosing products that are locally sourced, organically produced, or made with renewable resources, we contribute to a cycle of sustainability that lessens harm to our planet.

3. Engage in Community Action: Alone, our efforts may make a small impact, but collectively, our voices and actions can lead to significant change. Participating in or organizing community clean-up events, tree-planting drives, or conservation projects invigorates our collective mission. This doesn't only fate change at a local level but also nurtures a sense of community and purpose.

4. Integrate Prayer and Reflection: It is crucial to integrate prayer and spiritual reflection into our environmental efforts. Prayer opens our hearts to divine guidance, reminding us of God's presence in all creation. By dedicating time to reflect on the natural world, we enhance our awareness of its intrinsic value and the urgency of our protective roles.

5. Cultivate an Ecological Conscience in the Young: Education should not only inform but also inspire. Children and young adults must be guided in understanding their interconnectedness with nature. Educational programs that incorporate both scientific study and spiritual reflection prepare future generations to respect and safeguard the environment. This moral foundation encourages sustained ecological practices.

In fostering these practices, shared responsibility becomes evident. The Church encourages dialogue and cooperation among nations, institutions, and peoples to address environmental issues that transcend borders. This requires us to embrace solidarity and the common good, recognizing that every action reverberates globally. Building a culture of care necessitates addressing socio-economic systems that exploit the Earth and deepen inequality.

The intersection of faith and action finds its greatest expression when we view ecological efforts as evangelizing opportunities. Through our dedicated stewardship, we bear witness to the sanctity of life and creation, offering a testament to faith that speaks louder than words. These acts of care not only preserve the Earth but also transform hearts.

In conclusion, answering the call to care for God's creation encompasses embracing our God-given role as stewards. By committing to practical, compassionate actions supported by an informed conscience, we build a future where faith and sustainable living intertwine. This mission, profound in purpose yet simple in execution, beckons us to see each act as a step closer to a world that respects both its Creator and creation.

Chapter 9: Fields of Catholic Apologetics

As we delve into the expansive domain of Catholic apologetics, it becomes essential to survey the diverse fields through which the Catholic faith is articulated and defended. This chapter endeavors to illuminate the multifaceted nature of apologetics, where historical context, scriptural interpretation, philosophical reasoning, and moral discourse intersect to form a rich confluence that speaks to both the intellect and the spirit. In navigating these fields, we recognize the Church's tradition of engaging with seekers and skeptics alike, employing a rigorous yet empathetic approach that seeks to unveil the truth inherent in faith. This pursuit is not merely an academic exercise but a deeply rooted mission to share the inexhaustible light of Christ in every era. In continuing this journey, scholars and theologians are invited to explore the historical underpinnings of apologetic thought while considering its application in contemporary discussions, setting the stage for the more specialized forms of apologetics addressed in subsequent chapters.

Introduction to Catholic Apologetics

In an era drowning in opinions and philosophies, Catholic apologetics stands as a formidable bulwark, illuminating the truths of the faith amidst a myriad of shadows. It seeks to employ reason and revelation in harmony, guiding seekers from doubt to understanding. This field exists not to argue for the sake of argument but to unfold, with both humility and conviction, the splendor of the truth revealed through Christ and His Church. It invites both the skeptic and the believer alike to explore the depths of faith that doesn't merely withstand inquiry but embraces it.

Catholic apologetics, at its heart, is an intellectual and spiritual endeavor dedicated to defending and explaining the faith. Its roots trace deeply into the Church's rich tradition, standing on the shoulders of giants like St. Augustine and St. Thomas Aquinas, who adeptly utilized philosophy and theology to articulate the tenets of Christianity. Apologetics is not merely a reactive stance against criticism or secular assumptions; rather, it is proactive, eagerly engaging with questions and doubts that arise in the minds and hearts of both believers and non-believers. The aim is not only to affirm and protect the teachings of the Church but also to make them intelligible and relevant to contemporary society.

Within this dynamic domain, apologetics must draw upon various disciplines to meet the modern challenges it faces. This involves interfacing with history, philosophy, science, and culture, creating a comprehensive network that upholds the Church's teachings while addressing misconceptions and objections. The modern apologist must be versatile, capable of defending the faith against both old criticisms that persist and new ones that emerge from advances in science and shifts in culture. This breadth of engagement underscores the need for a rigorous and adaptable apologetic method.

As we begin this journey into the field of Catholic apologetics, it's crucial to understand the foundational principles that guide an apologist's work. Firstly, apologetics is deeply rooted in the belief that reason and faith aren't opposing forces but complementary paths leading to the same truth. This synergy places the apologist in the unique position of utilizing reason to support faith's mysteries, which transcend human understanding yet do not contradict it. Integrating philosophical reasoning with theological doctrine, apologetics articulates why belief in God, the divinity of Christ, and the teachings of the Church are not only reasonable but essential.

Moreover, Catholic apologetics must embrace a spirit of charity. The apologist's role is not simply to win arguments or prove others wrong; the ultimate goal is to guide others into a deeper relationship with God. Every encounter is an opportunity for evangelization, where the apologist becomes a vessel of God's truth and love, embodying Christ's teaching with sincerity and humility. Effective apologetics necessitates a deep understanding of the audience, addressing their doubts and nurturing their curiosity without judgment.

Another pivotal element is the balance between proclaiming objective truth and respecting the subjective journey of individuals. Apologetics insists on universal truths, but it also acknowledges personal experiences and queries. It aims to be a bridge, connecting people's lived experiences with the eternal truths of Catholic doctrine, encouraging individuals to see how the teachings of the Church illuminate their own lives. This empathetic approach fosters dialogue rather than division.

Within this framework, the task of the Catholic apologist becomes clear: to articulate the faith with both clarity and compassion in a way that resonates in today's world. This involves not just defending doctrines but doing so in a manner that speaks to the heart as well as the mind. It requires an understanding of the current intellectual and cultural climate, recognizing the influences that shape people's perceptions of faith. By doing so, the apologist can provide meaningful answers to the questions and concerns encountered in these contemporary contexts.

Apologetics, therefore, is an invitation to explore the mysteries of belief without fear. It reaffirms that faith is not contrary to reason but fulfills and transcends it. By engaging with apologetics, both the seeker and the believer can delve into richer understandings of the doctrines that sometimes appear lofty or abstract, bridging the gap between head and heart. This journey through Catholic apologetics is more than theoretical discourse; it's a practical exploration aimed at enriching one's faith journey and contributing to the mission of the Church.

In conclusion, Catholic apologetics serves as a crucial component in articulating the truth and beauty of the Catholic faith. It embodies the Church's commitment to reason and dialogue, meeting the world with love and truth. By fostering an authentic understanding of its principles, Catholics are better equipped to engage others in meaningful discussions about faith and life. As we proceed, we delve deeper into specific fields, whether historical, philosophical, or cultural, aiming to equip today's apologists with the necessary tools to carry forward the eternal mission of the Church in an ever-changing world.

Historical Apologetics

In the vast and intricate history of Catholic apologetics, the field of Historical Apologetics emerges as a cornerstone. This discipline seeks to anchor the Catholic faith in the verifiable events of history. By delving into the past, historical apologists provide a robust defense of the faith, addressing claims and misconceptions about the Church's history, its figures, and its institutions. While seemingly academic, the enterprise holds profound spiritual significance because it connects believers and skeptics alike to the historical reality of Jesus Christ and the Church he established. In a world often skeptical of unverified narratives, Historical Apologetics serves a crucial role in affirming the truth of Catholic doctrine through evidence.

Consider, for instance, the historical evidence for the life, death, and resurrection of Jesus Christ. These events are foundational to Christianity and, by extension, the Catholic faith. Historians both secular and religious have amassed a wealth of documents that attest to Jesus' existence and the transformative impact of his ministry. The Gospels, though theological in nature, are based on historical events witnessed by contemporaries. External sources such as the writings of Josephus and Tacitus further corroborate the Gospel accounts. For the Catholic apologist, these sources are not merely historical records; they are testimonies that underlie an unbroken chain of tradition and belief stretching back two millennia.

Yet, Historical Apologetics extends beyond simply documenting the life of Christ. It engages with various periods of Church history, addressing controversies, schisms, and moments of triumph and tragedy. The Crusades, the Inquisition, and the Reformation are often cited by critics as blemishes upon the Church's historical record. However, historical apologists seek not to whitewash these events, but to understand them in their full complexity. By doing so, they provide a nuanced view that acknowledges both human fallibility and divine providence. Figures like Saint Augustine and Saint Thomas Aquinas emerge as defenders and reformers, not immune to critique, but capable of offering profound insights into the human condition and the role of faith in history.

The task of the historical apologist also involves dispelling myths and misconceptions. Anti-Catholic narratives, such as those portraying the Church as an opponent of scientific progress, are refuted through evidence of the Church's substantial contributions to science, education, and culture. From establishing universities to preserving classical knowledge through the Middle Ages, the Church has played a pivotal role in the intellectual heritage of the West. Apologists illuminate these truths, revealing a narrative where faith and reason coexist harmoniously, each enriching the other.

Historical Apologetics is also deeply vested in the study of Church Councils, which provide insights into the development of doctrines and the Church's response to various heresies. Councils like Nicaea, Chalcedon, and Trent are pivotal moments where the Church, under the guidance of the Holy Spirit, clarified teachings that are central to Catholic doctrine today. Understanding the context and outcomes of these councils equips apologists with knowledge essential for defending the faith against reinterpretations and distortions of Church teaching.

Moreover, the field addresses the lives of saints and martyrs, those who have borne witness through their lives to the truth of the faith. These individuals are not merely historical figures; they are exemplars of living faith, bridging the gap between the mundane and the divine. Their stories, preserved through historic records, iconography, and hagiography, offer potent testimonies of the faith's transformative power. In bearing witness to the lives of such figures, apologists highlight the continuity of faith across time — from the Acts of the Apostles to the present day.

To engage effectively in Historical Apologetics, an apologist needs not just knowledge, but also wisdom and discernment. It involves understanding the subtleties and truths that lay beneath the surface of historical events and discerning how best to communicate these truths to a modern audience often steeped in skepticism. The tools of historical inquiry, textual criticism, and archaeological findings are wielded not as weapons, but as instruments of truth, helping to uncover the divine fingerprints throughout history.

Ultimately, Historical Apologetics offers a bridge between faith and reason, presenting Catholicism not as a relic of a bygone era, but as a living tradition informed by its past and relevant to contemporary life. It challenges us to appreciate the Church's history in all its richness and complexity, compelling us to see beyond the present and into the vast horizon of God's providential plan for humanity. In doing so, Historical Apologetics does not merely defend the Catholic faith — it celebrates it, inviting all to partake in the fullness of the truth found within the Church's historical witness. By understanding where we come from, we find clearer direction in where we are headed—towards a greater fulfillment in faith and understanding.

Chapter 10: Scriptural Apologetics

Scriptural Apologetics forms a critical nexus where faith and understanding meet, providing formidable defenses for the tenets of Catholicism by traversing the divine narrative of the Bible. In defending the faith through scripture, we uncover a rich reality where prophecy meets fulfillment, and allegory embodies truth, offering a basis for rational belief. The sacred texts are not merely historic relics but vibrant proclamations of God's eternal covenant with humanity. By embracing typology and realizing the echoes of Christ's passion in ancient stories, one witnesses the seamless continuity within the Scriptures that affirms the Church's teachings. Catholic scholars and apologists delve into key biblical defenses, from understanding the Church's foundation in the rock of Peter to the Eucharistic reality in John's Gospel. Each verse becomes a pillar, not just affirming faith but inviting skeptics to discover a coherent, divinely inspired mosaic where reason and revelation coexist. Recognizing scripture as both theologically profound and inherently practical, this approach not only reinforces Catholic doctrines but invites a renewed exploration of faith's intellectual depths within a skeptical world, all while fostering a lens of unity through divine love and wisdom.

Defending the Faith Through Scripture

In the grand life of faith, Scripture stands as a heartbeat enlivened with divine inspiration and human collaboration. It beckons us to dive deeper into its pages, not merely as passive observers but as active defenders of the faith it proclaims. For Catholic apologetics, Scripture isn't just a reference point; it is the foundation upon which we articulate and defend the tenets of our belief. This section, "Defending the Faith Through Scripture," calls us to understand, interpret, and proclaim the truths embedded within the Bible, doing so with a blend of intelligence, wisdom, and humility. Such an endeavor not only fortifies our faith but serves as a beacon to those who seek truth.

The Catholic Church holds that Scripture and Tradition are inextricably bound, forming a singular deposit of faith. To defend the faith through Scripture is to affirm this harmonious relationship, acknowledging that divine revelation is both written and unwritten. This dual approach is crucial for drawing skeptical minds into the conversation, emphasizing that the Word of God is living, dynamic, and relevant to our modern context. To navigate this, we must embark on a journey that respects historical context, linguistic nuances, and theological depth. Each passage becomes an opportunity to encounter Christ, who is both the giver of the Word and the Word Himself.

Central to our discussion is the understanding of Scripture as inspired. It is more than historical text or literary masterpiece. The Second Vatican Council's *Dei Verbum* reminds us that "Sacred Scripture is the speech of God as it is put down in writing under the breath of the Holy Spirit." This acknowledgment of divine authorship calls for a reading that transcends mere literalism. It invites us into a spiritual engagement that seeks the eternal truths God wishes to communicate. Amidst the contemporary clamor for scientific validation and historical accuracy, we assert that the truth of Scripture is not confined to empirical proof alone but is verified through the faith it nurtures and the lives it transforms.

A core challenge in scriptural apologetics is addressing apparent contradictions or difficult passages that skeptics might highlight. It is vital to approach these with both intellectual rigor and profound charity. The perceived inconsistencies often stem from a lack of understanding of the genres and contexts in which multiple biblical books were written. As apologists, our role is not to avoid these but to delve into deeper explanations, employing hermeneutics to unravel the layers of meaning embedded within the text. This necessitates a familiarity with the Church Fathers, whose insights still resonate with clarity and authority, guiding us towards sound interpretation.

Moreover, Scripture's defense involves elucidating its coherence with the broader spectrum of Catholic theology. This means demonstrating how doctrines of faith such as the Trinity, the Incarnation, or even the sacramental life are not merely devised concepts but are rooted in the biblical narrative. Opening the Bible through this lens reveals how unmistakably intertwined Scripture is with the Church's Magisterium. For instance, the

Eucharistic discourse in the Gospel of John doesn't exist in isolation; it is echoed in the early Church's liturgical practice and writings.

Addressing the question of sola scriptura—Scripture alone—as posited by some Christian denominations, provides an ample platform for captivating discussion. While Scripture is supreme, the Catholic perspective holds that it was never intended to function in solitude. Rather, it finds its fullness in conjunction with the Church's tradition and teaching authority. The Church, as the custodian of Biblical texts, also upholds the legitimate context in which they are to be understood. This ecclesial dimension is a testament to the communal and living nature of faith that spurs believers to encounter God profoundly both in Word and community.

When defending the faith through Scripture, the life and teachings of Jesus Christ, as depicted in the Gospels, take preeminence. Here, the apologist finds an inexhaustible well of wisdom and an embodiment of God's love. Christ's life functions as a vivid commentary on the Old Testament, fulfilling prophecies and establishing a new covenant. Understanding this typological relationship equips us to demonstrate Scriptural continuity and divine fidelity across both testaments.

The role of scriptural apologetics is not merely to convince but to engage with seekers on a journey towards the truth. Through compassionate dialogue and reasoned argument, the aim is to invite a movement from skepticism to belief. In engaging with those outside the faith, we adopt a posture of listening as much as articulating. This humble approach reflects Christ's own interactions, where questions were met, not with coercion, but with invitation.

Incorporating Scriptural apologetics into our personal spiritual life enriches our understanding and witness. Regular reflection and study, combined with prayer, allow Scripture to penetrate our hearts, making us living testimonies of its power. As we endeavor to defend the faith, we are reminded that the ultimate apologist is the Holy Spirit—guiding, illuminating, and sanctifying our efforts. In this endeavor, our mission is less about personal triumphs in argument and more about revealing the love of Christ to the world.

This section's exploration into scriptural apologetics sets the stage for practical defense strategies and deep theological insights in our ongoing quest to witness to the Roman Catholic Faith. Through discerning engagement with Scripture, we find not only defense but joy, wonder, and the profound presence of our Creator. As we proceed, let these words inspire us: "Always be prepared to give an answer to everyone who asks you to give the reason for the hope that you have" (1 Peter 3:15). In defending the faith, may we do so not merely with words but with lives illuminated by the light of the Gospel.

Key Biblical Defenses

Scriptural apologetics serves as a rich foundation for defending the Catholic faith. Within the vast narrative of the Bible lies an artifice of divine truth waiting to be unsealed. This task is both a privilege and a challenge, requiring an acute understanding of the text, tradition, and theological significance. The Catholic Church resonates with the belief that Scripture, while divinely inspired, doesn't stand in isolation. It is illuminated by the Sacred Tradition and authoritative teachings of the Magisterium. Together, they form a triad that defends and explains the Christian faith coherently and convincingly.

One of the most crucial aspects of scriptural apologetics is the authority of the Church itself. It's grounded in Matthew 16:18-19, where Christ declares Peter the rock upon which He'll build His Church. It's important to note that, in this passage, the promise of the keys to the Kingdom signifies authoritative teaching and governance. This founding scripture strengthens the Church's claim to apostolic succession and its interpretative authority over biblical texts, providing a sound response to those questioning the role of tradition in interpreting Scripture.

Moreover, the sacramental life of the Church finds its bedrock in biblical text. Take, for instance, the Eucharist, a cornerstone of Catholic belief and practice. The Sixth Chapter of John meticulously details Jesus' Bread of Life discourse, portraying the Eucharist not merely as symbolic but as a genuine participation in the physical body and blood of Christ. This passage is pivotal for presenting a compelling biblical defense of the real presence of Christ in the Eucharist—a truth venerable through the teachers and theologians of the Church.

Another key scriptural defense emerges in the doctrine of justification. It's nestled in the intricate theological interplay between faith and works, most notably discussed in James 2:24. The Catholic perspective asserts that a living faith, expressed through works, is necessary for salvation. Contrary to a mere forensic view of justification, the Church emphasizes an ontological change in the believer, made possible through faith and works. This balanced interaction provides a holistic understanding, challenging interpretations solely centered on faith apart from deeds, which some other Christian traditions hold.

Embedded within the Gospel of John is the profound mystery of the Incarnation (John 1:14), underscoring Jesus as the Word made flesh. This revelation serves as a bridge, offering a defense to the divinity and humanity of Christ. It's a central tenet that addresses various heretical beliefs by presenting Christ as fully divine and fully human, revealing the depth and breadth of His salvific work. Such clear biblical articulation ensures the Catholic position remains robust against reductionist interpretations, whether historical or contemporary.

The reverence for Mary, often a contentious point, also finds strong biblical roots. In Luke 1:28, the angel Gabriel greets Mary as "full of grace," an indicative statement of her unique role in salvation history. This scriptural acknowledgment of Mary's holiness provides a solid basis for Marian doctrines, including her Immaculate Conception and perpetual virginity. Far from detracting from Christ, the Church's Marian teachings highlight God's grace and underscore Mary's exemplary discipleship and cooperation with Divine Will.

Observing the vocation of the saints, the Epistle to the Hebrews describes a "great cloud of witnesses" (Hebrews 12:1), portraying the saints' lives as models of faith and perseverance. This text provides a solid case for the Catholic practice of venerating saints. It accentuates the communal and intercessory nature of the faith journey. Through their intercession, the faithful see the living manifestation of the Gospel in diverse paths, offering encouragement and guidance through varied life circumstances.

Finally, the prophetic and apocalyptic literature offers resources for apologetics concerning the end times and the Kingdom of God. The rich symbolism and visionary portrayals, notably in Daniel and Revelation, provide frameworks for understanding divine eschatology. They affirm the Church's teachings on the final judgment, resurrection, and the eternal reign of Christ. Through careful exegesis, these texts help Catholics articulate hope and trust in God's ultimate plan, challenging deterministic or nihilistic worldviews.

In navigating these biblical defenses, the Catholic approach is one of harmony—not isolating scripture from its tradition or theological context. The challenges faced by early Christians and resolved through scriptural interpretation and teaching councils continue to inform our methods today. By embracing both heart and reason, the Catholic Church invites theologians, scholars, and skeptics alike into a conversation that is as ancient as the faith itself, yet ever new in its presentation and defense.

Ultimately, addresses in scriptural apologetics are acts of faith and love. They are demonstrations of the hope the Church maintains—that the truth of God, revealed through Scripture, continues to speak powerfully to each generation. As apologists committed to this noble task, the responsibility remains to convey the enduring truth of Scripture in its fullness, ensuring that the sacred text shines as a beacon of wisdom across the centuries.

Chapter 11: Moral Apologetics

In the realm of moral apologetics, one stands at the intersection of ethical reasoning and divine insight, seeking to affirm the intrinsic dignity and moral framework of the Roman Catholic faith. This endeavor is not merely about defending doctrines but articulating a vision where morality is deeply intertwined with truth and love. As followers of Christ, we find our moral compass not only guided by natural law but also invigorated through the teachings of the Church, providing a coherent response to the moral objections skeptics often raise. Engaging with the rich tradition of Catholic moral theology involves a dual task: offering reasoned, philosophical foundations for our ethical stance while simultaneously pointing to the transformative power of grace that enables a genuine living out of these moral truths. Consequently, moral apologetics becomes a beacon, inviting skeptics and seekers alike to witness a life where the moral law is not a mere set of rules but a path leading to fulfillment and beatitude, grounded in the eternal wisdom and love of God.

Ethical Arguments in Apologetics

Moral apologetics serves as a vital tool in the arsenal of those who seek to articulate and defend the Roman Catholic faith. Its focus on ethical arguments provides a unique vantage point from which to address moral objections and affirm the cohesiveness of moral teachings within the Church. At the crux of this endeavor is the task of demonstrating that Catholic moral principles aren't merely abstractions, but rather, they are rooted in a deep understanding of human nature, divinely inspired truth, and the pursuit of the common good.

The task of moral apologetics is to reveal how Catholic ethical teachings align with a universal moral order. This order isn't arbitrary but is grounded in a vision of human flourishing that resonates with the deepest aspirations of the human heart. By persuading skeptics that Church teachings are not just reasonable but also profoundly humane, moral apologists strive to bridge gaps and dispel misconceptions that pervade modern discourse on ethics.

One central argument here concerns the objective nature of morality. In a world increasingly inclined towards moral relativism, the Catholic Church stands firm in its assertion that moral truths are not contingent on individual preferences or cultural norms. This conviction challenges the prevailing notion that ethical standards are merely social constructs, instead proposing that moral truths are immutable and universal, derived from God's eternal law. The Church's moral teachings, thus, represent a binding ethical framework applicable to all humanity, precisely because they echo this divine order.

Furthermore, moral apologetics addresses the perennial question of human dignity, elaborated extensively in Catholic social teaching. From the Catholic perspective, dignity is intrinsic, stemming from the belief that each person is made in the image and likeness of God. This understanding holds profound implications for modern ethical debates, ranging from the sanctity of life issues to the treatment of marginalized communities. Apologetics invites scholars to consider how this theological basis for human dignity stands in stark contrast to reductionist views that equate human worth with utility or productivity.

The Church's ethical vision extends beyond individual conduct toward communal responsibility. This notion of the common good is pivotal in navigating discussions of ethics within apologetics. Apologists articulate that pursuits of personal gain, when divorced from the well-being of others, fall short of the ethical life envisioned by Catholic doctrine. Moral teachings insist on balance—a harmony between personal fulfillment and communal welfare. It challenges individuals, especially skeptics, to envision a society built on solidarity and guided by principles like justice and charity, rather than solely personal satisfaction.

Moral apologetics doesn't merely engage abstract philosophical debates; it finds its application in the lived realities of Catholic practice. The rich deposit of Catholic ethical teachings provides nuanced guidance on diverse issues such as poverty, environmental stewardship, and social justice. Apologists must elucidate how Catholic ethics offer both profound insights and practical solutions to the ethical dilemmas facing contemporary society. For instance, when the Church discusses the option for the poor, it invites a radical reevaluation of societal values and economic priorities, advocating for proactive efforts to uplift the vulnerable.

Within the discourse of moral apologetics, the tension between divine law and human freedom often emerges as a significant theme. Some critics may argue that the Church's moral teachings constrain human freedom. However, Catholic apologetics seeks to reframe this perception, presenting these teachings not as arbitrary restraints but as pathways to authentic freedom. By aligning one's will with divine will, individuals are believed to attain not merely freedom from constraints but freedom for the good—the freedom to love as God intends. This paradox of freedom—finding liberation through adherence to moral truth—poses a challenge to contemporary views of autonomy.

Another facet of ethical arguments in apologetics involves tackling the problem of evil and suffering, a stumbling block for many in their faith journey. The Church's insights on the mystery of suffering offer a counter-narrative to nihilism and despair. By emphasizing redemptive suffering and the transformative power of grace, Catholic teaching provides a hopeful perspective, asserting that even in the midst of suffering, there exists a potential for spiritual growth and profound human goodness. Moral apologetics, therefore, encompasses a defense of Catholic beliefs about suffering as a gateway to deeper communion with God and others.

Furthermore, the Catholic ethical tradition places great importance on virtues, synthesizing them into the moral framework. Apologists are called to demonstrate how the cultivation of virtues like prudence, justice, fortitude, and temperance leads to a moral life that reflects the fullness of the Christian vocation. By embodying these virtues, individuals participate in a moral community that echoes the kingdom of God, illustrating the Church's moral teachings through their actions.

Ultimately, moral apologetics is not just about defending specific doctrines but about inviting others to a transformative understanding of ethical life within the Catholic tradition. It's an invitation to engage in the lifelong journey of conversion and holiness—a journey guided by truth and animated by love. The powerful synergy between ethical thought and heartfelt faith positions moral apologetics as a persuasive and essential facet of the Church's mission to articulate the faith in an ever-complex world. Through these arguments, apologists aim to illuminate the compelling integrity of Catholic morality, encouraging both believers and skeptics to embrace a coherent and meaningful vision of life guided by divine love and wisdom.

Addressing Moral Objections

When engaging in moral apologetics, perhaps the most pressing challenge lies in addressing the moral objections posed against the teachings of the Roman Catholic Church. Critics often question the Church's moral framework, exploring areas where they perceive inconsistencies, outdated doctrines, or potential conflicts with contemporary moral standards. To approach these objections effectively and convincingly, one must first understand the underlying principles of the Church's moral teachings.

A core tenet of Catholic moral teaching is the intrinsic dignity of the human person, rooted in the belief that each person is made in the image and likeness of God. This concept acts as the foundation for upholding moral norms relating to life, dignity, and freedom. However, as much as these principles guide our moral compass, they can also become a source of contention. Skeptics argue, for instance, about issues related to autonomy, such as reproductive rights and end-of-life choices, where Church teachings appear to limit personal freedom in favor of moral prescriptions, urging adherence to its understanding of natural law.

In addressing these objections, it's essential to delve into the concept of natural law, a pillar of Catholic moral theology. Natural law is seen as the intelligent order of creation, reflecting God's design and purposes. It suggests that moral truths are objective and discernible through human reason. However, when this ancient framework comes against modern interpretations of morality—often grounded in relativism and subjective experience—it invites a clash of paradigms. Thus, it's critical to articulate how natural law transcends mere cultural constructs and resonates with fundamental truths about human nature and flourishing.

Furthermore, Catholic moral apologetics must respond to critiques concerning the Church's stance on social justice and the treatment of marginalized groups. Recurring questions about historical events or perceived institutional failings expose a central concern: Is the Church living up to its moral ideals? The response lies not just in defending past actions but in demonstrating the Church's commitment to rectifying injustices and promoting human dignity through actionable love and charity.

Addressing the historical sins of the Institution—such as involvement or complicity in wars or discrimination—demands a posture of humility and repentance. Apologists can acknowledge these past failings without undermining the validity of Catholic truths. By highlighting periods of repentance and renewal, we affirm the Church's ability to grow and align more perfectly with its moral teachings. We also illuminate instances where Catholic social action has profoundly shaped human history, echoing its commitment to moral imperatives.

An intricate yet unavoidable moral objection concerns the perceived disparity between the Church's teachings on sexual morality and the increasingly diverse societal norms. This intricate dance entails explaining the Church's vision of human sexuality not as a rejection of physical love but as an embracing of its integrated purpose—enriching physical union with spiritual unity, ultimately within the sanctity of marriage. Critics often misinterpret this as a denial of human enjoyment or autonomy. Catholic teaching, however, proposes a more profound intimacy and freedom found within divine order.

Responding to these objections requires a recalibration of perspective: it is not a cold imposition of authority but an invitation to discover a life lived in accord with truth and beauty. Here lies an opportunity to frame moral teaching as not merely restrictive but liberating—accentuating the Church's view as a pathway to authentic love, joy, and fulfillment.

Ethical questions surrounding the Church's teachings on issues like contraception, LGBTQ+ relationships, and reproductive rights elevate discourse to ethical philosophy's heights. It's imperative to offer a comprehensive philosophical foundation that outlines why certain actions are deemed incongruent with human dignity. In doing so, we foster understanding, not merely of prohibitions, but of the profound "yes" the Church proclaims towards holistic expressions of love and fidelity.

In navigating contemporary societal friction points, it's crucial for Catholic apologetics to point toward the example of Christ, who personified love and truth. Unlike a rigid moralism, our apologetic task is to advocate a moral vision epitomized by compassion, which invites dialogue and encourages questions rather than suppresses them.

This approach isn't just doctrinal but profoundly practical. By emphasizing pastoral care, the Church shows genuine concern for the struggles people face in aligning lives with their deepest values. Moral apologetics, hence, futures balance between upholding immutable truths and fostering compassionate accompaniment, recognizing the journey each individual navigates.

Ultimately, addressing moral objections within Catholic theology requires more than curating logical arguments; it embraces living witness. The Church's moral teachings offer a comprehensive vision of human and divine relationships that should be visibly transformative. Through authentic lives dedicated to justice, mercy, and love, Catholic apologists have the most potent rebuttal to criticism: a beacon of hope that transcends mere words.

In conclusion, confronting moral objections calls us to articulate a moral apologetic that is intellectually coherent, pastorally sensitive, and authentically lived. It's a challenging but rewarding task, inviting all engaged in this dialogue to explore the depths of human dignity, the beauty of truth, and the possibility of lives fully aligned with divine love.

Chapter 12: Philosophical Apologetics

In the exploration of philosophical apologetics, we embark on a journey that melds reason with faith, an endeavor that is neither foreign to nor separate from the rich tradition of the Roman Catholic Church. Through the employment of logic and metaphysical inquiry, Catholic philosophical apologetics seeks to illuminate the rational foundation of faith, creating a dialogue where reason serves faith rather than opposes it. Rooted in centuries of thought, from the ancient musings of Aristotle to the systematic theology of Aquinas, these philosophical arguments advance a coherent, rational defense of the faith. By engaging with concepts such as existence, essence, and causality, apologetics finds a fertile ground upon which to construct arguments that are not only intellectually satisfying but also spiritually enriching. Thus, this chapter invites the skeptic and the believer alike to consider the harmony between faith and reason, which ultimately strengthens one's understanding and conviction of the divine mysteries housed within the Catholic tradition.

Utilizing Philosophy in Defense of Faith

Philosophical apologetics stands as a critical bridge between reason and faith, a dialogue between the temporal and the eternal. This section explores the profound ways philosophy can be employed to defend the Roman Catholic faith, leveraging millennia of philosophical thought. It's a realm where the truths of faith meet the principles of logic and reason, providing a robust framework for understanding Catholic doctrine. The integration of philosophy into theological discourse enriches our comprehension and allows for a deeper, more rational exploration of divine mysteries.

One of philosophy's quintessential roles is to serve as a tool for explaining and defending faith in a rational manner. The Catholic Church, with its rich intellectual tradition, has long utilized philosophy to clarify its teachings, offering reasoned responses to both skeptics and seekers alike. Philosophy provides language and concepts that can articulate complex theological ideas, making them accessible to those who may be distant from the faith. It's like a map that guides the mind through the intricate terrain of belief and doubt, illuminating the path to understanding.

Philosophers such as Augustine and Aquinas have demonstrated that faith and reason are not opposing forces but rather complementary ways of knowing. Augustine's works, for example, reflect a profound synthesis of Christian doctrine with Platonic philosophy, offering insights into the nature of God, the soul, and the moral law. This synthesis helped the early Church consolidate its teachings within the intellectual climate of the time, creating a legacy of philosophical theology that remains crucial today.

The concept of first principles, often explored in philosophical traditions, serves as a vital component in philosophical apologetics. These are fundamental truths that underlie other propositions or beliefs, offering a foundation upon which more complex understandings are built. For Catholics, the existence of God is a first principle. Philosophy allows us to explore this premise through various arguments, such as the cosmological, teleological, and moral arguments, each illustrating different facets of the divine's necessity and presence in our world.

Consider the cosmological argument, which asserts that everything that exists has a cause. This line of reasoning leads to the necessity of an uncaused cause, which we identify as God. This argument grounds the belief in God not only in faith but also in logical reasoning and empirical observations. By providing such arguments, philosophy equips believers with rational justifications that resonate with the intellect, complementing the spiritual convictions held in their hearts.

The moral argument, which considers the existence of objective moral values and duties, further exemplifies the power of philosophy. It posits that if objective moral values exist, there must be a moral lawgiver, who imbues creation with a sense of right and wrong. This idea counters relativism, a common philosophical objection to faith, by asserting the necessity of a divine moral order. The moral argument thus reinforces the Catholic understanding that God's laws are not invented but discovered through reason and conscience.

Equally compelling is the principle of sufficient reason, a cornerstone of rational inquiry that dictates every truth must have an explanation. The application of this principle within philosophical apologetics provides compelling evidence for God's existence, inviting skeptics to consider the logical necessity of a being that encompasses all truth and meaning. It challenges those who deny the validity of religious truth to provide equally rational explanations for the cosmos as is posited by theistic belief.

While philosophy aids in articulating the faith's rational basis, it also serves as a defense against the intellectual assaults on Catholic doctrine. In an age where scientific materialism and secularism often challenge theological claims, philosophy offers rebuttals that harmonize scientific knowledge with religious conviction. It shows that faith is not blind adherence but a reasoned assent to truths that transcend empirical evidence yet are not inherently contradictory to it.

Moreover, philosophical reasoning helps clarify and refine theological doctrines, pushing the boundaries of our understanding. For instance, the doctrine of the Trinity, a central mystery of the Christian faith, has been unpacked through philosophical discourse, employing language that, while limited, attempts to express the unity and distinction within God's nature. This intellectual endeavor facilitates a critical engagement with the faith, inviting believers to deepen their wisdom and skeptics to reconsider the coherence of Christian teaching.

In utilizing philosophy for the defense of faith, it's crucial to remain aware of the limitations of human reason. While powerful, reason alone cannot fully comprehend divine mysteries; it serves as a signpost pointing beyond itself. Philosophy, thus, becomes an entrance to deeper theological reflection, where faith enlightens the intellect, permitting a vision of divine truths that would otherwise remain veiled.

In conclusion, the role of philosophy in defending the Catholic faith is invaluable. It allows for the harmonious fusion of faith and reason, answering the call for a credible, rational expression of belief. By employing philosophy, Catholic apologists can effectively address the intellectual questions of the modern world, offering responses that are not only theologically sound but also intellectually satisfying. This ensures that the faith remains a living, dynamic force, capable of engaging with the complexities of contemporary thought while remaining steadfast in its foundational truths.

Major Philosophical Arguments

Within the realm of philosophical apologetics, major philosophical arguments stand as the cornerstones that support the intellectual edifice of Roman Catholic faith. In exploring these arguments, we delve into a tradition that, while ancient, remains vibrant and responsive to contemporary challenges. These arguments not only equip Catholic apologists with the tools to articulate and defend their faith but also invite skeptics into a reasoned dialogue with the beliefs and convictions held by the Church.

The first among these is the cosmological argument, often attributed to the thoughts of St. Thomas Aquinas. This argument posits that everything in existence is in motion and that motion must have been initiated by an unmoved mover, which Aquinas identifies as God. This argument addresses the eternal question of why there is something rather than nothing and suggests that the existence of a First Cause, unbounded by time and space, is necessary for the contingent realities we experience. It's a reflection on causality that draws on the observation of the natural world, resonating with those who see a harmony in the universe pointing toward a divine creator.

Next, we consider the teleological argument, also known as the argument from design. This perspective suggests that the order and purpose observed in nature imply the existence of a designer. The intricate complexities of life, the precise laws of physics, and the beauty of the cosmos speak to an intelligence that transcends mere chance. While critics may cite randomness or evolutionary explanations as counterarguments, the teleological perspective remains a profound testimony to those who see purpose woven into the fabric of creation. It challenges individuals to ponder the possibility that the universe's order is not accidental but intentional.

Another compelling philosophical argument is the moral argument, which argues for the existence of God based on the existence of objective moral values and duties. This line of reasoning suggests that if moral laws exist, there must be a moral lawgiver. In a purely materialistic world, objective morality would have little basis, as everything would be subject to personal or cultural opinions. Through this argument, Catholics assert that God provides the foundation for the morals that govern human life, leading to a profound discourse on law, justice, and ethical responsibility.

Furthermore, the ontological argument offers an intriguing approach to the question of God's existence. First formulated by Anselm of Canterbury, the argument posits that the very concept of a greatest conceivable being necessitates its existence in reality. It's a dense, abstract argument that has puzzled and inspired countless philosophers. Though some find it challenging, the ontological argument invites a deeper reflection on the nature of existence and the limits of human understanding in contemplating the divine.

The argument from religious experience should also be considered, appealing to those who value personal and experiential knowledge. This argument asserts that credible experiences of the divine reported by individuals across different cultures and times serve as evidence for God's existence. Though subjective, these experiences carry weight when considering the transformative power they exhibit in the lives of individuals. The argument underscores the belief that God is not merely a philosophical construct, but a living reality who engages personally with humanity.

Additionally, the argument from contingency and necessity plays a vital role in philosophical apologetics. It distinguishes between things that exist necessarily and those that exist contingently. The world we observe is filled with contingent beings that rely on external factors for their existence. This dependency suggests the existence of a necessary being, one whose existence itself is not contingent upon anything else. Such a necessary being provides an ultimate ground for all that is, leading Catholics to assert that God is this necessary being, sustaining creation through His very nature.

Lastly, the argument for the coherence of theism examines the internal logical consistency of the concept of God. This argument addresses concerns about contradictions within the religious understanding of divinity. It maintains that belief in God, particularly as understood in Catholic theology, is logically coherent and provides a comprehensive explanation of reality. This coherence reinforces faith by highlighting the logical integration of doctrinal elements, such as the Trinity, within the broader metaphysical framework of Christian teaching.

In summary, these major philosophical arguments together form a robust body of thought that equips Catholic apologists to engage with modern intellectual challenges while inviting skeptics into meaningful dialogue with the faith. They demonstrate that belief in God, as understood in the Catholic tradition, is not only a matter of faith but also one of reason and intellectual inquiry. Through these arguments, Catholics not only defend their beliefs but articulate a vision of reality that seeks to harmonize faith with reason in a coherent and compelling way.

Chapter 13: Scientific Apologetics

Within the realm of scientific apologetics, we find a profound intersection between faith and reason, a space where science becomes a partner rather than an opponent of Catholic doctrine. This chapter addresses the perceived discord between scientific discovery and religious belief, highlighting their compatibility through thoughtful dialogue and exploration of the natural world. Science, far from being an adversary, serves as a testament to the intricacy and magnificence of divine creation, providing Catholics with tools to articulate the faith's rational grounding. By examining the foundational compatibility of scientific inquiry and theological tenets, this discussion aims to dismantle common objections raised by skeptics. Through the lens of philosophical reasoning and empirical evidence, we find that the pursuit of truth in both fields leads to a deeper appreciation of the Creator's handiwork, inviting a harmonious coexistence that enriches both scientific understanding and spiritual insights.

Science and Faith Compatibility

Amidst the intellectual pursuits of humanity, science and faith often seem to traverse parallel paths. Yet, upon closer inspection, we find that these paths intertwine and support one another, weaving a tapestry that illustrates the complementary nature of both domains. In the context of Catholic apologetics, it becomes imperative to elucidate how science and faith, far from contradicting or negating each other, coexist harmoniously within the broader spectrum of truth and understanding.

The Catholic Church has long held that faith and reason are not only compatible but are essential partners in the journey toward understanding the natural world and divine revelation. This alliance finds its basis in the belief that all truth has a single source—God. As Vatican Council II articulated, faith and reason are "like two wings on which the human spirit rises to the contemplation of truth." This fundamental harmony mandates that scientific discoveries, when properly understood, can enrich and deepen our faith.

Scientific inquiry, with its rigorous methodologies and empirical foundations, provides us with profound insights into the workings of the universe. From the majestic dance of celestial bodies to the intricate mechanisms of living organisms, science reveals the beauty and orderliness inherent in creation. Such revelations do not diminish the role of faith. Instead, they magnify it, inviting believers to appreciate the magnificence of God's handiwork.

One might question whether tensions arise when scientific findings appear to conflict with religious teachings. Historical instances, such as the Galileo affair, often cast a shadow over the discourse on science and faith. However, these conflicts are frequently rooted in misinterpretations or limited understandings that evolve over time. The Church acknowledges the provisional nature of scientific theories and encourages their pursuit for the greater glory of God, thereby fostering an environment where open dialogue and exploration can occur.

The Church's embrace of science is evident throughout history. Many Catholic clergy and laypeople have made significant contributions to various scientific fields. Gregor Mendel, widely known as the father of genetics, was an Augustinian friar. Georges Lemaître, a Belgian priest, proposed the Big Bang theory, a scientific model describing the universe's origins. These exemplary individuals demonstrate that a robust faith in God can coexist with a profound commitment to scientific endeavors.

It is crucial to recognize that faith and science occupy different domains of inquiry, each with distinct methodologies and goals. Science seeks to understand the natural world through observation and experimentation, while faith deals with metaphysical questions of purpose, meaning, and morality. When we appreciate the scope and limitations of each, we provide a framework where they can coexist without encroaching upon or negating each other's realms.

The Catholic intellectual tradition emphasizes the unity of truth. This principle allows for a synergetic relationship between science and faith, whereby the truths uncovered by science complement and illuminate the transcendent truths revealed through faith. Such harmony invites believers to engage with the world intellectually and spiritually, fostering a holistic understanding of existence.

While the Church advocates a collaborative relationship between science and faith, it maintains a critical perspective when evaluating scientific findings. This discernment ensures that scientific interpretations align with the fundamental tenets of faith and moral teachings. It is not an instance of imposing faith upon science but rather a call to engage with science thoughtfully and ethically.

Today's rapid scientific and technological advancements pose new challenges and opportunities for this compatibility. Issues related to biotechnology, artificial intelligence, and cosmology require Catholic scholars to blend scientific knowledge with theological insights to address ethical and existential questions. By synthesizing these disciplines, the Church continues to offer a coherent vision that respects both the autonomy of science and the richness of faith.

Ultimately, the compatibility of science and faith serves as a testament to the coherence of Creation and the Creator. The vastness of the universe calls forth a sense of awe and wonder that transcends empirical explanation, inviting believers to ponder the mystery that underlies all existence. In this light, science becomes a vessel that transports us to the threshold of the divine, prompting reflections beyond the material realm.

One might say that science enriches faith by providing a deeper appreciation of God's magnificence, whereas faith infuses science with purpose, guiding the moral and ethical application of scientific knowledge. This dynamic interplay reaffirms our identity as both rational and spiritual beings, called to explore the unknown while remaining rooted in eternal truths.

Thus, Catholic apologetics must continue to foster a dialogue that articulates the compatibility of science and faith. Such endeavors not only defend the faith against misconceptions but also invite skeptics to explore the fullness of truth that encompasses both reason and revelation. This harmonious relationship provides fertile ground for apologetics, inviting questioning minds to see beyond dichotomous thinking and embrace a unified vision of truth.

In summary, science and faith find compatibility not in eliminating questions but rather in embracing complexity. The Church's commitment to this relationship echoes throughout its teachings and traditions. This synthesis invites all, whether believer or skeptic, to partake in a journey that seeks understanding through a lens of wonder, guided by the humility to acknowledge the mysteries that science unravels and the mysteries that faith elucidates.

Countering Scientific Objections

The relationship between science and faith has often been portrayed as a battleground, where each seems to launch objections and counter-objections across a seemingly insurmountable divide. Yet, discerning minds must recognize that the interplay between faith and reason is integral to a holistic understanding of truth. The Catholic Church, far from obstructing the advancements of science, has consistently held that both faith and reason emanate from the same divine source, and thus cannot truly contradict each other. Still, numerous objections arise from the scientific community that demand careful and thoughtful responses from Catholic apologists.

One common objection states that the Church's teachings are antithetical to scientific discoveries, particularly those concerning the origins of the universe and life itself. Critics often point to historical events, such as the Galileo affair, as evidence of an inherent conflict. However, to perceive science and the teachings of the Church as adversaries is to misunderstand the nature and purpose of both. The Church acknowledges that science has the capacity to explore and reveal the mechanics of the natural world, while theology addresses questions of meaning and purpose that transcend empirical observation.

Moreover, the Galileo case is more nuanced than typically portrayed. The Church's initial resistance was not purely ideological but was influenced by the scientific consensus of the time, which Galileo's heliocentric model challenged. Today, the Church acknowledges her missteps in handling the situation, and this historical lesson emphasizes humility and dialogue in engaging with scientific ideas. The Church has since supported scientific inquiry, understanding that genuine scientific discoveries can illuminate the divine hand in creation, much like the writings of Aquinas and Augustine, who long argued that God could be known through His creation.

A distinct scientific objection often raised concerns the theory of evolution, which some claim contradicts the account of creation in Genesis. The Church, however, does not insist on a literalist interpretation of Scripture. Instead, it holds that the divine truths conveyed in Genesis about God's creation and the inherent dignity of human beings coexist harmoniously with evolutionary theory. Pope Pius XII, in *Humani Generis*, and subsequent papal teachings have made it clear: evolutionary theory, when viewed through the lens of faith, points to the grandeur of God's creative work.

The doctrine of original sin presents another focal point of objection. Critics argue that if humans evolved, traditional understandings of original sin originating from a single pair of human ancestors become untenable. Yet, the Church's philosophical frameworks enable an understanding of original sin as a reality that coexists with evolutionary biology. Cardinal Ratzinger, later Pope Benedict XVI, suggested that we can understand original sin through the narrative lens of symbols representing profound truths about humanity's relationship with God, rather than as a historical account alone.

Moreover, the question of miracles continues to spark debate. From a strictly scientific stance, miracles pose a contradiction, as they represent phenomena that seemingly defy natural laws. However, for believers, miracles do not undermine science but reveal God's ability to intervene in creation. St. Thomas Aquinas offered profound insight, positing that miracles are not contra to nature but are, instead, acts of God that surpass the ordinary workings of nature. Recognizing the limits of scientific explanation and the mystery that faith embraces is crucial here.

In addressing these objections, Catholic apologists must utilize reasoned arguments to show that the assertion of scientific authority does not eclipse theological truths. They should emphasize that science and faith investigate different dimensions of human experience and should engage in mutually enriching dialogue. By affirming that spiritual and empirical truths coexist, apologists can demonstrate the integrative power of the Catholic worldview.

A central task involves countering the caricature of faith as merely an appeal to blind belief. The Church teaches that faith is rationally grounded and that believers are called to seek understanding. Science, restricted to what is measurable and observable, cannot speak to metaphysical realities. Apologists should therefore articulate how faith provides answers to the ultimate questions of purpose and existence that lie beyond science's empirical scope.

Furthermore, in addressing the advances in fields like neuroscience and artificial intelligence, which challenge notions of free will and consciousness, Catholics should assert the philosophical underpinnings of these concepts. The Church posits that while science may describe processes of the brain, it cannot fully account for the human soul's intricacies. By fostering collaborations with scientific disciplines, Catholic scholars have the opportunity to bridge the gap and offer profound insights into human nature.

Therefore, in countering scientific objections, Catholic apologists have the profound task of presenting a vision where faith and science enrich rather than contradict each other. Engaging with scientific theories—be they about the cosmos, biological evolution, or human psychology—through the lens of faith becomes an exercise not in conflict but in complementarity, revealing a deeper, richer system of truth.

Thus, the Catholic apologist must cultivate the delicate art of dialogue, eloquently articulating not only the Church's teachings but also a sincere openness to scientific discovery. It is in this space that the Church's faith in both God's revelation and humanity's rational capacity finds its most compelling witness—a hopeful reminder that truth, wherever it is found, ultimately leads to God.

Chapter 14: Historical Apologetics

In examining the historical apologetics of the Roman Catholic faith, one must delve into the depths of tradition and history that illuminate the authenticity and resilience of Catholic beliefs. This realm of apologetics seeks to present compelling evidence for the faith through the lens of historical continuity and truth. Historical evidence provides a framework for understanding how the Church has been guided and preserved throughout the ages, despite the ebbs and flows of time and culture. The encounters of saints, the Councils' decrees, and the unwavering consistency in doctrine offer a profound testament to the Church's divine origin and mission. Beyond merely defending the faith, historical apologetics invites skeptics and believers alike to witness a narrative shaped by divine providence. By addressing misconceptions and debunking historical myths, this approach endeavors to showcase how the faith, supported by historical moments and figures, stands not only as a relic of the past but as a living testament to truth. This chapter encourages both heart and mind to engage with history, fostering a deeper connection with the Church's rich heritage and its unyielding testament to faith. Consider this an invitation to explore how the light of history casts an indelible glow on the path of belief through the centuries.

Historical Evidences of Faith

The journey of faith is interwoven with the ceaseless march of history. For those who seek understanding, the Roman Catholic Church presents an abundant plethora of historical evidences that articulate the divine truths entrusted to it. From the outset, Christianity has been a faith firmly rooted in historical events, and its continuous thread can be traced through the lived experiences of those who've sought to embody the teachings of Christ.

Early accounts of the Christian faith are grounded in the testimonies of the Apostles and their immediate successors. These bearers of the Good News, emboldened by their direct experiences with Christ, formed the backbone of the nascent Church. The foundational texts, traditionally attributed to various Apostles and evangelists, reflect not merely theological aspirations but accounts deeply embedded in specific historical contexts. The gospels and epistles serve not only as spiritual guides but also as historical documents that provide insights into the social, political, and religious landscapes of the first century.

Historical evidence for the faith extends beyond the written word. Archaeological discoveries continually affirm and illuminate the settings and events described in these early writings. From the ancient city of Ephesus, where Saint Paul was said to have preached, to the humble dwelling in Bethlehem, where tradition holds that Christ was born, these tangible remnants of the past provide a bridge between scripture and reality. These sites, their artifacts, and the cultures unearthed contribute layers of authenticity to the historical narrative of Christianity.

Moreover, the martyrdom of early Christians stands as a powerful testament to the veracity and profound impact of the Christian message. The innumerable accounts of individuals who willingly faced persecution and death rather than renounce their faith paint a vivid picture of conviction and demonstrate the transformative power of Christian belief. Their sacrifices are captured not only in textual records but also in the remains of catacombs and ancient relics that immortalize their steadfast faith.

The doctrine of apostolic succession provides another compelling line of evidence for the historical continuity of the faith. Catholic tradition holds that the authority of the Church has been passed down unbroken from the Apostles through successive generations of bishops. This lineage is more than a mere clerical roster; it's a tangible link to Christ Himself, grounding contemporary Catholicism in the teachings and practices of its earliest practitioners. Documents, such as the works of Saint Irenaeus and Eusebius, carefully trace these successions, offering a genealogical assurance of doctrinal integrity.

Throughout the centuries, ecumenical councils have played a critical role in shaping and preserving Church doctrine. These councils comprise another layer of historical evidence, documenting the Church's responses to theological dilemmas and heresies. From Nicaea to Chalcedon to Trent, the councils' decrees bear witness to the Church's commitment to maintaining orthodoxy and unity. The preserved proceedings and their subsequent implementations manifest a coherent tradition that navigated the complexities of evolving historical contexts.

In addition to texts and councils, the Catholic Church has produced a rich patrimony of sacred art, architecture, and liturgy, all of which serve as historical markers of faith. From the grandeur of St. Peter's Basilica to the stained glass windows of Chartres, these creations are not merely aesthetic triumphs but embodiments of theological and historical narratives. They stand as testaments to the generations who have expressed their faith through creative genius and to communities united in worship and purpose.

- The Church's art holds within it allegories and symbols that convey complex theological truths in ways words alone often cannot. Such art immerses the believer in a sensory experience of divine realities.

- Architectural marvels such as cathedrals and monasteries symbolize the Church's enduring presence and are historical records of the faith's influence on culture and society.

The miraculous, too, forms a significant component in the historical evidences of faith. Reports of unexplainable healings, apparitions, and other signs are abundant in the Church's tradition. While skeptics might challenge these occurrences, their investigation, documentation, and recognition by the Church follow rigorous scrutiny. The Lourdes and Fatima apparitions, for instance, are etched into Catholic consciousness, offering hope and testament to the supernatural dimension of the faith.

Yet historical apologetics is not merely about defending past events; it is about understanding how continuously unfolding history affirms the faith's timeless truths. Even in the face of historical challenges, whether through political upheaval, scientific advancements, or cultural shifts, the Church has responded with resilience. It seeks not to diminish the truths of other disciplines but rather to integrate them into a comprehensive understanding of reality that points ultimately to its divine origin.

Catholic theologians draw upon historical evidence not as an end in itself but as part of a complex and living faith tradition that seeks truth in all its forms. The interpretation of this evidence aims to enhance understanding and foster dialogue with the broader world. As history reveals the unfolding of the divine drama, the Catholic faith continues to articulate its message—a message deeply rooted in historical certainty and ever relevant to contemporary challenges.

Debunking Historical Myths

Within the realm of historical apologetics, the task of addressing and correcting misconceptions is essential. These myths, often perpetuated by misunderstanding or misinterpretation, can cloud the true essence and historical realities of the Catholic Church. In this section, we aim to dissect some of the most prevalent historical myths, thereby elucidating the Church's authentic role and influence through history. This endeavor not only clarifies theological truths but also preserves the dignity of the Church across eras.

One of the most enduring myths is the notion that the Middle Ages, often pejoratively referred to as the "Dark Ages," were a period of cultural and intellectual stagnation. This metaphorical darkness is frequently attributed to the Church's influence, suggesting it stifled progress and inquisitiveness. However, a closer examination reveals a vibrant era marked by the establishment of universities, the flourishing of Scholastic philosophy, and significant advancements in art and architecture, most notably through the Gothic cathedrals. Far from being a barrier to intellectual inquiry, the Church was a chief patron of this vibrant intellectual life.

Another widely circulated myth is that of the Church's active opposition to scientific advancement. Critics often point to the case of Galileo Galilei as emblematic of a wider anti-scientific sentiment. However, this oversimplifies a complex narrative. The Church has historically been a supporter of the sciences, fostering an environment where inquiry and faith coexist. The Gregorian Reform, the establishment of medieval universities, and the contributions of clergy like Georges Lemaître, who proposed the Big Bang theory, underscore the Church's long-standing relationship with scientific inquiry.

The myth of the Crusades as a purely aggressive and imperial initiative by the Church often oversimplifies the historical context. While undeniably complex and not without its moral failings, the Crusades arose from a confluence of political, religious, and social factors that cannot be solely attributed to a singular motivation. The call for crusade was also a response to centuries of Islamic conquests that threatened Christendom's Eastern territories, and it was perceived at the time as a defensive action.

Furthermore, the Spanish Inquisition is frequently portrayed as a symbol of unchecked ecclesiastical tyranny, yet historical evidence suggests a more nuanced reality. While abuses did occur, they were often exaggerated by opponents of Spain and the Church. Modern scholarship reveals that the Inquisition was relatively restrained compared to contemporary secular European courts, and it provided the accused with more rights than was typical elsewhere.

There is also a common belief that the Church, throughout history, has been uniformly opposed to progress and reform. Contrary to this belief, it has been an agent of cultural and moral evolution at pivotal moments, including the adoption and promotion of human rights, notably influenced by Church teachings on the inherent dignity of the human person. These principles were instrumental in shaping Western legal traditions, underscoring human rights and the common good.

An additional myth involves the supposed widespread illiteracy sanctioned by the Church. In reality, monasteries were central hubs of knowledge, scribes painstakingly preserved and copied texts from antiquity, creating libraries and fostering learning. This myth overlooks the Church's crucial role in education and literacy, seen through early schools such as those founded by Charlemagne's reforms, which emphasized literacy and learning.

Myths about the alleged misogyny of the Church need careful reevaluation. Historical records show the veneration of female saints and the notable influence of convents as centers of learning and spiritual authority. Women like Hildegard of Bingen and Catherine of Siena held significant religious power and influence, contradicting simplified narratives of systematic oppression.

Finally, it's essential to challenge the myth that the Catholic Church has universally resisted democracy and freedom. Enlightenment critiques often painted the church as antithetical to liberty, yet Catholic social teaching has long emphasized the dignity of the individual and the importance of social and political structures that enhance the common good. The work of papal encyclicals, like Rerum Novarum, highlights the Church's alignment with social justice and democratic ideals.

In unraveling these historical myths, we are reminded of the importance of a disciplined approach to history—one that is willing to confront uncomfortable truths but equally ready to recognize complexity and nuance. Misconceptions often arise from a tendency to impose contemporary values and frameworks on historical contexts that were vastly different from our own. Debunking these myths requires a balanced reading of history and an understanding of the Church as an ever-evolving institution that is both divine and human in its journey through time.

The task of apologetics, therefore, goes beyond mere defense; it seeks to uncover the truth behind the layers of misunderstanding that time and prejudice can construct. By addressing these myths head-on, Catholic apologists are not just safeguarding the Church's past but also reinforcing a well-founded faith built on historical reality and theological truth. Through this endeavor, we invite others to explore the historical Church not as a relic of dogma, but as a living, breathing testament to faith intertwined with the course of history.

Thus, the path of historical apologetics, with its commitment to truth, justice, and the defense of our faith against unwarranted claims, remains as vital today as it has always been. By correcting misconceptions, we honor the past, inform the present, and inspire the future, inviting all to witness the comprehensive truth of the Catholic tradition.

Chapter 15: Cultural Apologetics

As we navigate the intricate dance between faith and contemporary culture, cultural apologetics emerges as an essential discourse for engaging with modernity while remaining rooted in timeless truth. The Roman Catholic tradition offers a rich system through which believers can address the often tumultuous confluence of art, literature, music, and societal norms with the core tenets of Christianity. This chapter explores how ancient wisdom can respond to the existential queries posed by today's secular milieu, providing a dialogue marked by both reason and faith. By approaching culture not as an adversary but as a field ripe for engagement, Catholics can gracefully articulate the relevance of their beliefs, transforming perceived conflicts into opportunities for evangelization. Through cultural apologetics, we not only defend the faith but also touch the human heart, inviting the skeptic to see the world anew through the lens of divine love and purpose, highlighting the harmonious relationship between the secular and the sacred.

Engaging Modern Culture

Our cultural endeavor as Catholics calls us to engage with modern culture, not simply to survive in it but to illuminate it with the light of our faith. This task, delicate yet profoundly important, involves articulating the truths of Catholic teaching in a way that resonates within the shifting paradigms of contemporary society. It requires a grasp of both the essence of our faith and the languages of the current cultural milieu. The world in which we live is marked by rapid change, varied worldviews, and unprecedented access to information. It is in this environment that cultural apologetics must find its voice.

Catholicism has always found ways to speak to the heart of the culture it finds itself in, from the early Church Fathers conversing in Greek philosophy to St. Thomas Aquinas synthesizing Aristotelian thought with Christian doctrine. Today, this engagement must be just as innovative and relevant. We need to draw from our rich theological traditions while also harnessing new tools and mediums that technological advancement has made available. The challenge is to maintain fidelity to the truths of our faith while speaking in a language that contemporary culture can understand and appreciate.

Central to engaging modern culture is the concept of dialogue. It is not enough to merely speak truth; we must engage with the questions and concerns of our time with charity and understanding. In an age where information is abundant yet often superficial, we have the responsibility to offer depth and meaning. Dialogue involves listening as much as it does speaking and demands a respect for the legitimacy of questions posed by skeptics and seekers alike. Through genuine engagement, we create an opportunity for conversion, both of hearts and minds.

Modern culture is deeply influenced by secularism and relativism, ideologies that often run contrary to the absolute truths upheld by the Catholic Church. To engage effectively, we must confront these ideologies head-on, offering coherent and compassionate responses. Secularism may promote a worldview void of the divine, but our role is to articulate the inherent longing for transcendence that resides within every human heart. Likewise, the relativism that dismisses absolute truth as unattainable is met with the robust intellectual tradition of the Church which confidently proclaims truth's existence and knowability.

In our engagement, we must not shy away from utilizing the arts and sciences as allies rather than adversaries. Art, in its myriad forms, speaks a language that often transcends intellectual argument and reaches the emotive core of human experience. Similarly, the natural sciences, far from disproving religious beliefs, reveal the ordered beauty of creation that points toward an intelligent Creator. By integrating the truths of faith with the findings of science and the beauty expressed in art, cultural apologetics becomes a dynamic and attractive mode of evangelization.

Moreover, in an age characterized by narratives of independence and self-sufficiency, the Catholic narrative of community and interdependence speaks volumes. The Church's teachings on the common good and solidarity challenge the prevailing cultural norms of individualism. By presenting the Church as a loving community that cares for the marginalized and vulnerable, we counter narratives that promote isolation. This embodiment of love and service becomes a powerful witness to the world.

It's crucial, however, to approach these cultural engagements with humility and empathy. Arrogance or an attitude of superiority will alienate those we wish to accompany on their journey of faith. Instead, we must embody the virtues of patience and understanding, demonstrating through our actions a profound respect for the dignity of every person, regardless of their beliefs or background. Through this approach, we pave the way for authentic dialogue and mutual enrichment.

We live in a world where the digital realm holds immense influence. Social media, podcasts, and digital forums have become modern-day agoras where ideas are exchanged and debated. As Catholic apologists, entering these spaces offers immense potential for evangelization but also requires discernment and adaptability. The digital environment can amplify both truth and falsehood; thus, we must be vigilant in maintaining integrity and charity in our communications. Striving for clarity and kindness, we can leverage these platforms to build bridges and foster understanding.

Ultimately, our engagement with modern culture must be rooted in love—a love that mirrors Christ's own love for humanity. This love forms the foundation of all apologetic endeavors, transforming them from mere intellectual exercises to acts of profound witness. As influencers of culture, we are called to be both thoughtful and courageous, offering the riches of our faith in a way that transforms not only individual hearts but the world around us.

The success of cultural apologetics cannot be measured in numbers but rather in the depth of impact. It may be a single conversation, an essay read online, or an art exhibit that invites a viewer to see the world through a new lens, all contributing to a cumulative effect that nourishes the soul of culture with the life-giving truth of the Gospel.

In conclusion, engaging modern culture as Catholic apologists is an ongoing journey, necessitating continuous learning, adaptation, and reliance on the Holy Spirit. Our mission is to remain steadfast in our faith while offering compelling reasons for others to embark on their own journeys toward truth. By doing so, we participate in the Church's enduring call to be a light to the nations, guiding our modern world toward the ultimate truth of God's love for all His creation.

Faith in the Modern World

In the bustling agora of modern life, where ideas clash and narratives intermingle, the place of faith is often questioned. It's within this vibrant and often chaotic context that we must examine the role of Catholic faith and its ability to thrive amid contemporary challenges. The world has transformed in ways unimaginable to our forebears, yet the essence of truth and moral understanding remains timeless. The task of cultural apologetics, then, is not only to defend the faith but to reveal its profound relevance right here and now.

The modern world presents unique challenges to the notion of faith. In an age dominated by materialism, where existential queries are often overwhelmed by daily distractions, it is easy to disassociate from the spiritual dimensions of life. Modernity, with its technological advancements and secular ideologies, seems to pose an antagonistic front against religious belief. However, this perceived opposition is, in truth, an opportunity for deeper engagement. The Catholic Church, with its rich tradition, speaks to the core of human experience and offers answers to questions that remain unspoken in the public sphere.

To engage modern culture effectively, we must first understand its narratives. The predominant narratives often revolve around autonomy and relativism, characterized by the idea that truth is subjective and self-defined. Against this backdrop, Catholicism proposes a universal truth anchored in the divine. The Church's teachings provide a counter-narrative that addresses the innate longing for meaning and connection found in every human soul. This isn't a battle of ideologies but a journey toward discovering a deeper truth that transcends transient cultural shifts.

Catholic apologetics, in addressing the modern world, must be rooted in an understanding of both faith and reason. The notion that faith and science, faith and logic, faith and empirical evidence are adversely aligned is a fallacy long discredited by the Church's scholarly traditions. Rather, they are allies in the pursuit of truth. An eloquent apologist must be well-versed in the language of modern discourse, able to translate ancient wisdom into contemporary contexts without diluting its essence. It calls for a harmony of tradition and innovation, reflecting a Church that lives within the present while rooted firmly in its timeless foundation.

Moreover, the existential questions of meaning, purpose, and destiny have never been more pertinent. Modern life may offer the illusion of answers through technology and fleeting pleasures, yet the human soul craves more profound sustenance. The teachings of the Church speak to this need, offering a vision of life that is rich in purpose and guided by love and charity. In the crowded marketplace of ideas, the Catholic faith provides not just answers but a comprehensive narrative that encompasses both the seen and unseen, the physical and metaphysical.

The art of Catholic apologetics in a modern context involves not only defending but also illustrating how faith enriches human life. This requires an engagement with culture, not as an opponent but as a field ripe for sowing seeds of understanding and wisdom. The

Resilience of faith has been proven time and again throughout history; it has faced down empires, withstood marauding critics, and emerged renewed from within its own challenges. Today's landscape may be unfamiliar, but the Church's mission remains unchanged.

Contemporary skeptics often highlight the apparent rigidity of religious dogma as a hindrance to human freedom. Yet the paradox is that true freedom is found within the bounds of truth, a truth that faith reveals. The sacraments, liturgy, and doctrine of the Church are not mere relics of a bygone era but are vibrant, living conduits of grace and freedom. This counterintuitive assertion demands an apologetic approach that is not only logical and historical but personal and transformative, illustrating through lived examples and testimonies how Catholic faith elevates the human experience.

There is, in the heart of every skeptic, a yearning for truth—a yearning that is often masked by layers of doubt and the chaos of modern life. Cultural apologetics must therefore embrace empathy and understanding. It's not enough to present arguments; one must listen, engage, and walk alongside those who question, affirming their search for meaning while guiding them towards the light of faith. The journey to belief is a profoundly personal one, and the apologist serves as a guide, patient and enduring, reflecting the compassionate patience of the Church herself.

In engaging faith within the modern world, a dynamic approach is necessary. This includes recognizing the common ground shared by all humans, regardless of their belief systems, and building upon it. The love, compassion, and justice that the Church teaches resonate deeply within human hearts across cultures and epochs. It becomes imperative to highlight these universal virtues, demonstrating how they find their fullest expression within the tenets of Catholic faith.

Ultimately, the practice of cultural apologetics is not about winning debates but winning hearts. It's about opening dialogues, fostering relationships, and cultivating an environment where faith can take root and flourish amid the complexities of modern life. This approach is not dogmatic but relational, recognizing that faith is lived in community and grows in the soil of human interaction.

The modern world, with all its intricacies and challenges, is not a barrier to faith but a frontier. It is ripe with potential for those willing to articulate the timeless message of the Church in terms that resonate today. As Catholics, our mission is to engage with this world—not retreat from it—proclaiming a faith that is as relevant in the fleeting opportunities of now as it was in the earliest days of the Church. Through reasoned persuasion, compassionate action, and unwavering witness, the Catholic Church continues to offer the world a vision of faith that transcends time, deeply rooted in love and inexhaustible in its capacity to transform the human heart.

Chapter 16: The Seven Virtues

The seven virtues form a cornerstone of Catholic moral teaching, providing a framework for living a life that mirrors divine grace and aligns with the highest moral ideals. Encompassing both the theological virtues—faith, hope, and charity—and the cardinal virtues—prudence, justice, fortitude, and temperance—these qualities offer a blueprint for personal development and societal harmony. By embracing these virtues, individuals are drawn closer to God, fostering a spiritual equilibrium that transcends mere adherence to rules. This transformative journey requires the active cultivation of habits that orient the intellect and the will towards good, enabling believers to withstand the pervasive temptations of vice. In this chapter, we'll explore how to understand and live out these virtues in daily life, witnessing to the faith with a steadfast heart and a discerning mind. Infused with divine assistance, the virtues serve not just as moral guidelines, but as the path to sanctity and a profound expression of love in action.

Understanding the Virtues

In the rich tradition of Catholic theology, the virtues hold a unique and vital place. They are not merely abstract ideals but are foundational to living a life aligned with Christian principles. The virtues serve as navigational stars guiding the faithful through the moral and spiritual complexities of human existence. They are rooted deeply in both scripture and tradition, providing a stable framework upon which to build a life of grace and holiness.

What are virtues? At their core, virtues are habitual and firm dispositions to do good. They enable individuals to not just perform good acts but to give the best of themselves. The virtuous person tends toward the good with all his sensory and spiritual powers; he pursues the good and chooses it in concrete actions. The importance of understanding virtues cannot be overstated, as they are the bedrock of moral theology, setting the stage for the development and deepening of the moral life.

Let us explore the classical distinction between the theological virtues and the cardinal virtues. The theological virtues—faith, hope, and charity—are gifts from God that empower the believer to participate in God's divine nature. These virtues are foundational to the Christian calling, planting the seeds of divine life within us. They orient us directly toward God, who is the ultimate end of virtue and happiness.

Meanwhile, the cardinal virtues—prudence, justice, fortitude, and temperance—are pivotal in regulating moral conduct. Known as the "hinge" virtues, they are so called because they play a central role in guiding other virtues. Prudence helps us discern our true good in every circumstance and choose the right means of achieving it. Justice facilitates giving both God and neighbor their due. Fortitude strengthens us amid difficulties and temptations, while temperance enables us to control our desires and seek balanced fulfillment of our appetites.

Understanding these virtues requires engaging with the very questions of what it means to be human and how to cultivate a life that not only resists vice but actively seeks holiness. Each virtue, whether theological or cardinal, functions like individual pieces of a larger mosaic, contributing uniquely to the complexity and beauty of Christian life. It's not enough to merely know these virtues but to integrate them actively in one's journey toward sanctity.

Furthermore, the virtues challenge us to transcend our natural tendencies. The struggle against sin and vice is framed not as a mere negation of bad behaviors but as the active cultivation of virtue. For each vice, there exists a corresponding virtue that manifests the positive aspects of what it means to live in alignment with God's will. Understanding virtues, therefore, becomes a dynamic process, one of growing into the fullness of human potential as envisioned by divine providence.

One might ask, why is such a deep understanding of the virtues necessary? Within the Roman Catholic context, virtues do more than improve individual moral character; they fortify communities, churches, and societies. In reflecting the likeness of Christ more vividly, one becomes a beacon of grace, influencing others toward truth and goodness through example. The virtues are fundamentally communal as much as they are personal, demonstrating that our moral choices resonate far beyond the boundaries of personal existence.

The anchoring of virtues in both scripture and tradition offers rich material for theological reflection and practical application. The catechism of the Church heavily emphasizes virtues as essential to living a Christian life. However, to truly grasp the transformative power of virtues, one must look to the lives of the saints, who showcase the virtues in their radiant splendor—turning to them not only for inspiration but for intercession and guidance.

The interplay between virtues and vices further enriches our understanding. For each virtue actively pursued diminishes the power of vice, replacing darkness with light. This dynamic reveals a deep psychological and spiritual truth—that weaknesses and sins are opportunities to practice and grow in virtue. It's a testament to the redemptive power of grace, which elevates human effort to align more closely with divine will.

In philosophical terms, the cultivation of virtue is itself a path to happiness. St. Augustine famously posited that our hearts are restless until they rest in God, and it is through the virtues that we orient our restless hearts toward the divine. St. Thomas Aquinas added to this discourse, systematically defining each virtue and its function within the moral life, embedding them within the broader framework of natural law and divine grace. The intellectual pursuit of understanding these virtues becomes not just an academic exercise but a quest for the good life itself.

Critically, the virtues offer a stable moral compass in an ever-shifting cultural landscape. In a world that often confuses success with virtue, the traditional Catholic virtues provide clarity, offering enduring guidelines that resist the shifting sands of societal trends. They stand as timeless reminders that true human flourishing is not found in indulging every desire but in mastering oneself through the practice of these age-old truths.

Ultimately, the study and understanding of virtues transcend the realm of theological reflection, entering into lived experience. As Catholics, embracing and living out these virtues reinforces the core belief in humanity made in the image of God and destined for greatness beyond earthly life. The virtues, then, are not just concepts but lived realities, shaping character and destiny, guiding each soul toward its ultimate end in union with God.

Living Out the Virtues

To live out the virtues is to engage in a deliberate and continuous act of conforming one's life to divine law, as understood through the teachings of the Catholic Church. This process demands an awareness of the virtues not merely as abstract concepts but as practical guides to human behavior. Each virtue acts as a beacon, guiding one towards a life that reflects the values of the Kingdom of God, embodying the principles of charity, humility, and justice. Yet, while the virtues stand as cornerstones of Catholic living, the journey to authentically embody them requires both wisdom and perseverance.

The challenge, of course, lies in the application of the virtues in the everyday fabric of human existence. In a world fraught with moral ambiguity and confrontation, the virtues serve as a compass, offering direction amid the shifting sands of modern morality. Courage, for instance, is not merely the absence of fear but rather the ability to hold steadfast to the truth amidst adversity. Similarly, prudence involves the discernment of the right course of action at the right time, a skill increasingly vital in our fast-paced, ever-evolving society.

In the realm of virtue, action and contemplation go hand in hand. The contemplative dimension involves a deep engagement with God's word and the sacramental life, which nourishes the soul and aligns the mind towards truth. Reflecting on the examples of saints, who lived their lives centered around these virtues, can inspire and fortify our own commitments. These holy men and women were not without fault or struggle; instead, they persisted, continually drawing strength from their faith.

However, living out the virtues isn't a solitary endeavor. It's deeply interwoven with community life. Through communal worship and mutual support, individuals find encouragement and accountability in their pursuit of holiness. The Church, as a body, cultivates an environment where virtues can take root and flourish. This ecclesial context provides both a refuge and a point of reference where the faithful can engage more fully and effectively with the virtues in practice.

Let's consider the virtue of justice. Justice demands that we render to others what is rightfully theirs, transcending more than legal obligation and entering into the moral framework of human dignity. It invites us to evaluate our relationships and societal structures critically. Justice calls one to be an advocate for those marginalized, ensuring that their voices are heard, and their needs are met. The Catholic social teaching principles of human dignity and the common good amplify this virtue, urging the faithful to extend it beyond personal interaction into the larger social fabric.

In contrast, the virtue of temperance speaks to the balance and moderation necessary in personal desires and actions. It ensures that neither excess nor deficiency governs one's life. In today's culture, where indulgence often eclipses restraint, temperance serves as a counter-cultural statement affirming the human capacity for self-control and harmony. By embracing temperance, individuals nurture inner peace and contentment, the fruits of a life rightly ordered.

The pursuit of these virtues leads one towards an integrated life, where faith and action align. This integration isn't automatic but requires intentionality and reflection, often through ongoing conversion and reformation of the heart. While one might persistently aim for virtue, the reality is that human frailty can lead to failure. The sacrament of reconciliation plays a crucial role here, offering the grace needed to rise again and renew one's effort to live virtuously after a fall.

In an ever-complex world, living out the virtues can illuminate paths that align with God's will, shaping not only personal lives but also influencing family, community, and society at large. Each act of virtue contributes to creating a culture rooted in divine love and truth. As such, virtues become tools for transformation, allowing the faithful to be catalysts for change and healing in the broader world.

Ultimately, the journey of embodying the virtues is one of faithfulness to the Gospel. Faith, seen as both a virtue and gift from God, both initiates and sustains this pilgrimage of life. In faith, one finds the impetus to act justly, love mercifully, and walk humbly with God. Faith doesn't operate in isolation but is dynamically expressed through hope and charity—the theological virtues that unify and elevate the cardinal virtues.

Living out the virtues reflects a continual process of aligning oneself with the divine, striving to embody Christ's love in all things. While imperfection marks every human effort, grace abounds, providing strength where weakness lies. In embracing this, the faithful not only fulfill their personal calling but also witness to the world the transformative power of a virtuous life centered on God's vision for humanity.

Chapter 17: Faith, Hope, and Charity

In the symphony of virtues, faith, hope, and charity stand as resounding chords that harmonize the believer's journey toward divine unity. Faith, the cornerstone of our spiritual architecture, calls us to trust in the unseen and embrace the mysteries of God's promises, leading us not by the clarity of human reason alone, but by a profound assent to divine revelation. Hope, meanwhile, acts as the anchor for our souls, grounding us in the unwavering expectation of eternal beatitude and sustaining us through life's tempests by fostering a resilient spirit that yearns for the everlasting joy God has promised. Yet, it is charity that crowns the theological triad, transforming belief and expectation into action. This sublime love propels us toward God Himself, manifesting in acts of self-giving that reflect the divine love poured into our hearts by the Holy Spirit. Together, these virtues orient the intellect and will towards the ultimate good, encouraging a life of grace that not only sees but feels and acts in accordance with the divine will. As we traverse the path of earthly existence, the cultivation of faith, hope, and charity offers an intrinsic guide, a roadmap that not only draws us towards the heavenly realm but transforms the world here and now into a testament of God's eternal kingdom. Through them, we embody the transformative power of the Gospel, engaging both the believer and skeptic in a journey of love that fulfills the law and the prophets.

Deep Dive into Theological Virtues

The theological virtues—faith, hope, and charity—are fundamental to the spiritual life within Roman Catholic theology. These virtues are considered gifts from God, infused into the souls of believers. Unlike the cardinal virtues, which can be developed through human effort, the theological virtues are bestowed upon us by divine grace, allowing us to partake in God's own nature. They orient us towards God in a profound way, shaping our entire moral and spiritual existence.

Faith is typically the bedrock of theological virtues, and it's much more than mere belief or intellectual assent. In the Catholic tradition, faith is an act of trust and commitment to God. It engages not just the mind but the will and heart. Through faith, one enters a personal relationship with God, accepting His divine revelation as truth. St. Thomas Aquinas described faith as the virtue by which we are disposed to assent to whatever God has revealed solely because of the authority of God revealing it. In this respect, faith transcends the purely rational as it leads to a deeper understanding of truths that are not accessible by reason alone.

Hope is the second cornerstone and acts as the anchor for the soul. It's not a simple optimism or wishful thinking but a steadfast trust in God's promises. Hope invites us into a future-oriented mindset, guiding us to eternal bliss and encouraging us to persevere through trials. It is the virtue that sustains the believer through despair and tribulation. Hope provides courage and directs our desires towards ultimate fulfillment in God, warding off the crippling tendencies of despair and presumption. In a world filled with uncertainties, hope acts as a beacon, shining the light of divine assurance onto our paths.

Charity, or love, is perhaps the greatest of the theological virtues, often encapsulated in the phrase "God is love." In the language of the New Testament, charity is the 'agape'—a selfless, divine love that wills the good of the other for the sake of the other. It's dynamic, outward-focused, and is profoundly action-oriented. Charity cultivates loving relationships with both God and neighbor, embodying the commandment to "love one another as I have loved you." It completes and perfects the other virtues, for it is through charity that we fully participate in God's divine nature.

The interconnectedness of these virtues is significant; each supports and enhances the others. Faith lays the groundwork for hope; without believing in God's promises, hope would have no foundation. Charity, in turn, is nourished by faith and hope, as it directs our lives entirely towards God and others. In Catholic theology, these three virtues coexist in harmony, forging a pathway for personal sanctification and communal transformation. They are crucial in the spiritual battle against sin and help align our will with divine intentions.

Moreover, these virtues exemplify an essential understanding of Catholic moral theology, differing fundamentally from those conceived in mere humanistic terms. They assert that divine assistance is necessary for true moral perfection. No human effort can attain the heights of these virtues without divine grace collaborating with human freedom. The theological virtues offer a profound response to the existential concerns that preoccupy many skeptics and seekers. They invite an engagement with a metaphysical reality that transcends earthly limitations.

Faith, therefore, demands not only an assent to divine truths but also invites believers into a relationship characterized by trust and fidelity to God's commandments. This relationship is nurtured by the Church's sacramental life and her teachings. The Catholic Church argues that faith should not be isolated or seen as an individualistic venture but should be practiced within the community of believers. This communal aspect reinforces one's faith as members support and encourage each other to remain steadfast.

Hope stands as the virtue amidst adversity, encouraging believers to remain optimistic about the victory of grace. In Catholic eschatology, hope becomes especially poignant. Believers look forward to the resurrection of the dead and life in the world to come. Such hope shapes how Catholics live today, influencing their decisions and behavior. It imbues them with a sacrificial, forward-looking attitude, aligning earthly actions with heavenly expectations.

Charity, the crowning glory of the virtues, manifests in concrete acts of kindness and service. It transforms social relations, fostering peace, justice, and forgiveness. Charity is not mere sentiment but is intrinsically tied to the will and to action. In theological terms, it becomes the measure by which one's closeness to God and neighbor is gauged. Therefore, acts of charity are integral to Catholic identity and mission.

In conclusion, the theological virtues are vital in the discourse of Catholic apologetics. They articulate a unique understanding of the relationship between God and humanity, addressing the profound questions of existence, morality, and divine destiny. For the theologian and skeptic alike, these virtues challenge us to explore the depths of divine love, redefining what it means to live a virtuous life. Through faith, hope, and charity, we are called to more than mere ethical living; we are invited into a transformative communion with God.

Chapter 18: Prudence, Justice, Fortitude, and Temperance

Moving from the theological virtues discussed previously, we now stand before the cardinal virtues: prudence, justice, fortitude, and temperance. These virtues, acting as the hinges (or "cardo" in Latin) upon which moral virtue pivots, are fundamental to living a life of integrity and balance. Prudence guides our practical reasoning, enabling us to make decisions aligned with God's will. Justice propels us to give God and our neighbor their due, illuminating our path toward righteousness. Fortitude instills in us the courage to endure trials and pursue goodness against adversity. Finally, temperance aids us in moderating our appetites, allowing us to enjoy God's creation without falling into excess. Together, these virtues orchestrate a harmony within our moral framework, bridging our human frailty with divine grace. In practicing these virtues, we reflect God's image, encouraging a life that not only honors Him but also draws others towards truth and virtue, as we weave them into the fabric of daily life through conscious and deliberate action.

Exploring the Cardinal Virtues

The cardinal virtues—prudence, justice, fortitude, and temperance—serve as the cornerstone of moral philosophy within the Catholic tradition, forming the bedrock of a virtuous life. These virtues are not merely abstract ideals but practical guides for living in accordance with God's will. As we delve into the significance of each, we shall see how they intertwine to sculpt a life of moral integrity that aligns with the natural law imprinted upon human hearts. Their cardinal nature implies a 'hinge' upon which all moral virtues depend, a concept richly explored by Saint Thomas Aquinas who synthesized Aristotelian philosophy with Christian doctrine.

Prudence, often regarded as the "charioteer of the virtues," plays a critical role by enabling individuals to discern our true good in any given situation and to select the right means of achieving it. It's not mere shrewdness or cunning; rather, it is a wisdom that engages both moral insight and careful deliberation. Practically speaking, prudence demands that we think rightly about actions, integrating reason and memory while also being open to counsel. In its divine light, prudence helps us perceive the eternal truths and act upon them within temporal affairs. The prudent person is one who evaluates circumstances, learns from past experiences, and places each decision within the grander narrative of God's eternal law.

In contrast, justice concerns itself with the moral quality of our relationships with others. It is the virtue that inclines us to give each person their due, which surpasses mere legal obligations. Aquinas emphasizes that justice is fundamentally about the right ordering of relationships, allowing communal harmony and ensuring that love, as Christ commands, is actualized in every facet of human interaction. From a theological perspective, justice is inherent to God's character and, therefore, deeply rooted in divine law. This virtue extends beyond the interpersonal to embody the broader notions of social justice, compelling believers to challenge societal structures that undermine the dignity of the human person.

Fortitude, on the other hand, equips the individual to face difficulties and trials with a steadfast spirit. It is more than mere physical courage; it embodies a resilience that enables one to pursue the good, even in the face of fear, pain, or adversity. The Christian understanding of fortitude is intrinsically linked to the hope of eternal life, allowing believers to withstand temporary suffering for the sake of a greater, eternal reward. Fortitude finds expression in the martyrs' witness—a testament to the power of divine grace as it bolsters the soul against seemingly insurmountable odds. It calls us to align strength with moral conviction, ensuring that courage is not reckless but rooted in righteousness.

Finally, temperance serves as the moderating influence, ensuring that our desires and passions remain aligned with reason. It is a discipline of self-control, not as a form of deprivation, but as a path to true freedom. True temperance creates harmony within the soul, enabling individuals to desire what is good and shun excesses that lead to vice. In our contemporary context—amidst a culture often characterized by excess—temperance is particularly challenging and counter-cultural, yet it is vital. Temperance, therefore, is not about the extinguishing of desire, but about channeling it toward what is noble and eternal.

Each of these virtues performs a specific role but cannot function in isolation; they are interconnected and inform one another. For instance, prudence guides justice by determining what is fair in specific contexts, while temperance and fortitude ensure that justice is pursued with the right amount of passion and resolve. Together, they construct a moral framework that not only elevates individual character but also fosters the collective well-being. The practice of these virtues becomes a form of living out the Gospel, showing a skeptical world the coherence and beauty of the Catholic moral teaching.

The cardinal virtues prompt deep reflection about the purpose of human life and we must articulate them convincingly to engage skeptics. They aren't archaic relics but relevant guides, linked intimately with Catholic social teaching and the Church's vision for human flourishing. Emphasizing these virtues is also essential for apologetics as they offer a rational, philosophical defense of the faith that appeals to both heart and mind. This makes them indispensable tools for those endeavoring to present a cohesive, compelling case for Christianity in modern discourse. The life of virtue, as illustrated by these cardinal virtues, invites us into a richer, fuller humanity—a testimony to the transformative grace offered through the Catholic faith.

Practical Applications of Cardinal Virtues

The cardinal virtues of prudence, justice, fortitude, and temperance serve as the foundation of moral character in Catholic teaching. These virtues are not lofty ideals meant to be appreciated only by theologians and scholars. Instead, they find their true significance in the everyday actions and decisions of the faithful. Such virtues guide us in our pursuit of living a life that reflects the teachings of Christ, advocating for human dignity, and promoting the common good while acknowledging our fallibility.

Prudence, often described as practical wisdom, is the ability to judge correctly what is right and what is wrong in any given situation. It serves as the charioteer of the virtues, directing other moral qualities by discerning the appropriate course of action. In the daily life of a Catholic believer, prudence can guide decisions at all levels—be it in corporate leadership or within the intimacy of family choices. A prudent leader, for instance, weighs the company's financial goals against its ethical responsibilities to community and ecology. He seeks not only profit but aligns business strategies with the preservation of human dignity and environmental stewardship.

Prudence empowers individuals to navigate complex social issues with clarity. In a world awash with information, the prudent person discerns what is truly beneficial and what may be misleading. This doesn't just apply to mitigating harm but extends to actions that proactively uplift and support societal well-being. The virtue thereby bridges the gap between moral consideration and action, serving as a practice ground for other virtues. Without prudence, the potential for justice may never transition into reality because the means to achieve it remain unconsidered.

Turning to **justice**, this virtue pertains to giving each individual their due. It is a call to fairness, not merely in legal terms, but as a fundamental ethos shaping our interactions with others. Justice ensures that love for one's neighbor manifests in tangible forms—work that pays a living wage, policies that protect the vulnerable, and advocacy for those who suffer under unjust systems. Within a family, justice means equitable sharing of resources, attention, and emotional support.

In the public square, justice manifests itself in our calls for social reform. When advocating for the poor, justice helps us transcend charity, pushing towards changes that address systemic causes of poverty. Practical justice encourages voting for laws that align with Catholic teaching by balancing individual freedoms with societal responsibilities. The pursuit of justice is unending and dynamic, requiring constant reflection and action to align with new understandings and challenges.

Fortitude, the virtue of courage, provides the mental and emotional strength necessary to face difficult situations. It is commonly tested in one's willingness to stand for truth, justice, and faith, even amidst opposition. This can occur in both monumental decisions, like taking a moral stand that might lead to persecution, and smaller, everyday acts such as remaining faithful to one's ethical standards despite societal pressure to conform.

Practical applications of fortitude are evident in the quiet perseverance required to live out one's vocation. A teacher dedicating her life to educational justice in underfunded schools exhibits fortitude. A medical professional working in resource-poor settings, prioritizing patient care over financial gain, relies equally on this virtue. In these instances, fortitude helps maintain resolve, reinforcing the belief that good will triumph, though it might not always be immediate or visible.

Temperance, often mistakenly thought of solely in terms of moderation concerning physical goods, extends to all areas of life where control and balance are essential. It encourages restraint and balance, reminding us not to act on impulse or desire alone. This balance stretches beyond personal moderation in food and drink—it includes managing emotional responses and material possessions.

In contemporary society, temperance is counter-cultural. It guides individuals to live authentically and sustainably, eschewing rampant consumerism and environmental exploitation. Practicing temperance may mean resisting the allure of the latest technological gadgets or fashion trends to focus resources on more meaningful, lasting endeavors. In a family setting, temperance nurtures harmony by fostering an environment where listening and patience prevail over quick judgments and heated arguments.

In conjunction, these virtues create a framework upon which a faithful life is built. They invigorate moral development and civic responsibility. A person who cultivates these virtues becomes a beacon of integrity in both ecclesiastical and secular spaces. They embody teachings that aren't merely adhered to but are lived out visibly, impacting communities around them.

These applications highlight how the cardinal virtues permeate all strata of life, shaping not only personal holiness but societal transformation. They encourage sacrifice for a greater good, instill respect for others' rights, and inspire actions that conform to God's will. As Catholics, implementing these virtues becomes the foundational means through which we enact our faith, bearing witness to its transformative power. In achieving this, our convictions foster societies that mirror divine love, where human dignity is preserved, justice prevails, courage thrives, and balance is honored.

Chapter 19: The Seven Vices

The path to virtue is marked not merely by the choice of good but also by the conscious rejection of vice, as the seven vices stand opposed to the flourishing of the soul in harmony with divine will. Pride, the queen of sins, exalts self above God, leading to the fall of angels and men alike. Envy distorts appreciation into resentment, corrupting the good possessed by others. Greed shackles the heart to material abundance, replacing the divine with the temporal. Gluttony, in its excess, drowns spiritual hunger in transient satiation, while lust, a distortion of love, seeks the fleeting over the eternal. Anger, unchecked, scorches charity, leaving ashes of discord in its wake. Finally, sloth, insidiously cloaked in apathy, neglects both divine calling and earthly duty. Recognizing these vices is crucial in the spiritual journey, for only by acknowledging our moral ailments can we earnestly seek the remedy offered through the sacraments and the transformative grace of God. This struggle, both internal and communal, mirrors Augustine's "City of God," where the earthly and heavenly realms contest the affections of humanity. By naming, understanding, and overcoming these vices, we align ourselves more closely with the virtues that reflect the image of our Creator, and thus prepare ourselves for the ultimate fulfillment of our purpose in Him.

Analyzing the Vices

In our quest to navigate the moral landscape outlined by Catholic doctrine, we encounter the provocative terrain of the seven vices. These vices, often misunderstood as mere moral failings, are deeply rooted in both theological reflection and human experience. They serve as a cautionary guide to the pitfalls that threaten the spiritual and ethical life of Catholics. To understand these vices more profoundly, we must delve into their origins, manifestations, and the subtle ways they weave into human behavior.

The concept of the seven vices—or "deadly sins" as they're sometimes referred to—dates back to early Christian teachings. These vices are: pride, greed, lust, envy, gluttony, wrath, and sloth. Each one represents an exaggerated or distorted virtue, leading the soul away from divine love and towards selfishness and spiritual decay. Through the ages, the Church Fathers and theologians have grappled with these vices, providing insights that are as relevant today as they were centuries ago. The enduring relevance of this moral framework lies in its ability to diagnose the ailments of the soul, guiding believers towards a more virtuous life grounded in faith.

Pride, often deemed the root of all vices, can be seen as an inordinate self-love that places the self above all else. It entails a rejection of one's proper relationship with God and others. This vice blinds individuals to the necessity of grace and humbles service in the Christian life. Pride distorts our perception of self-worth and fosters a false sense of independence from the Creator. Greed, or avarice, follows close behind as the excessive desire for wealth and material possessions, eroding the space within us that should be reserved for the generosity of spirit.

Lust is understood as a disordered desire for sexual pleasure, pursued for its own sake, thereby divorcing it from its intended purposes within the bonds of love and procreation. Lust objectifies others, reducing human dignity to mere physicality, and engenders relationships built not on mutual respect and love, but on self-serving desire. Envy, a vice born from comparing ourselves unfavorably to others, denies the unique gifts and graces bestowed upon each individual by God. It can breed resentment and division, eroding comunitas and the unity of the Church body.

Gluttony extends beyond mere over-consumption of food; it is an inordinate preoccupation with indulging the senses, ignoring the call to temperance. This excessive attachment to the material renders one less receptive to the spiritual hunger that truly sustains us. Wrath, or intense anger, similarly disrupts the peace intended by divine order. It is often irrational, destructive, and difficult to control, leaving a trail of broken relationships and spiritual scars in its wake.

Finally, sloth embodies spiritual and physical laziness, a disregard for duties and responsibilities. It curtails one's capacity to engage with both God's creation and personal vocation. Sloth is more than mere laziness; it signals a languishing spirit that has forgotten or refused to respond to the love and call of God.

Understanding these vices involves recognizing their subtlety. Rarely do they appear overtly or fully formed. Instead, they often manifest in seemingly innocuous thoughts or desires, gradually gaining strength if unchecked. This insidious growth requires vigilant reflection and self-awareness. It calls for us to examine our consciences regularly, to discern where these vices take root, and to call upon divine assistance in curbing their influence.

In our analysis, it is crucial to acknowledge that vices are not inexorable. With the guidance of the Holy Spirit and a commitment to the sacraments, especially confession, believers can develop the virtues that counteract these vices. For instance, humility combats pride, charity counters greed, chastity moderates lust, kindness extinguishes envy, temperance governs gluttony, patience quells wrath, and diligence overcomes sloth. Each vice finds its antidote in the corresponding theological and cardinal virtues.

The pedagogical aspect of analyzing vices involves both self-learning and communal edification. Through engaging with these teachings, believers can deepen their understanding of human nature and the perpetual struggle between good and evil. Such knowledge serves as a bulwark against despair and a guide towards the hope that God's grace is ever-present, enabling transformation and redemption.

The Church, through her pastoral care and the wisdom of her saints, offers numerous resources for those seeking to overcome these vices. Spiritual direction, prayer, and meditative reading of Scripture are invaluable tools in this spiritual journey. Furthermore, the lives of saints serve as testament to the possibility of overcoming vice through faith and perseverance.

In conclusion, the examination of the seven vices is indispensable for fully apprehending the Roman Catholic moral tradition. It invites not only an understanding of the vices themselves but a comprehensive view of the human condition and its potential for sanctification. By charting a course through these moral challenges, the faithful are better equipped to live a life that mirrors Christ's love and reflects the image of God imprinted on each of us. Through continual reflection, community support, and divine grace, the journey towards virtue becomes not just a duty, but an enriching pilgrimage into deeper union with God. Analyzing these vices, therefore, is not merely an academic exercise, but a profound spiritual endeavor crucial for the flourishing of one's soul.

Overcoming the Vices

In the journey toward moral and spiritual maturity, confronting the vices that plague humanity is not only a challenge but also an imperative. Within Catholic teaching, these vices, often referred to as the "seven deadly sins," form a framework of moral obstacles that, left unchecked, can lead the soul astray. The path of conversion calls for a conscientious effort to overcome these vices through both divine grace and human endeavor.

The first step in overcoming any vice is recognition and acknowledgment. It requires an honest self-assessment, a keen awareness of one's own frailties and tendencies toward evil. Pride, often considered the root of all vices, is particularly insidious. It blinds one to personal faults, making it difficult to seek help or transformation. Yet, the antidote lies in humility—a virtue that opens our eyes to the truth of our condition and encourages a sincere return to God. Embracing humility allows us to reorient our lives towards a higher goal, serving as a counterforce to pride's corrosive effects.

Each of the vices—greed, lust, envy, gluttony, wrath, and sloth—has its own countering virtue that serves as a beacon for overcoming it. Greed, with its insatiable desire for more, is tempered by the virtue of generosity. Through acts of charity and self-giving, one can slowly dismantle the fortress of materialism that greed seeks to build. Similarly, chastity acts as the protective barrier against the destructive power of lust, fostering love that is pure and selfless rather than selfish and objectifying.

Envy often leads to resentment and bitterness; it is a poison to the soul that eats away at one's happiness and peace. Gratitude, therefore, becomes a powerful tool in overcoming envy. By cultivating a spirit of thankfulness, we shift our focus from what we lack to the abundance of what we have, recognizing all as gifts from God. The practice of regularly expressing gratitude transforms our perception, aligning us with the divine will rather than human comparison.

Gluttony, in its pursuit of indulgence and excess, dulls the senses and obscures spiritual insight. Fasting acts as both a sacrifice and a discipline that counteracts gluttony. Through fasting and moderation, we learn to control bodily desires, freeing the spirit to seek nourishment in God instead of in ephemeral pleasures. The hunger that fasting instills becomes a longing for divine sustenance, aligning us more closely with our true essence.

Wrath, or uncontrolled anger, often causes irreparable harm to relationships and communities. Patience and forgiveness create a pathway through which wrath can be managed and reformed. By practicing these virtues, we learn to respond to provocations with a calm and measured spirit. This approach not only restores peace but fosters healing where anger might have sown discord.

While sloth seems harmless in its passive form, its true danger is in its ability to paralyze the will and stifle spiritual growth. Diligence and zeal reignite the soul's passion for good work and draw it out of lethargy. By cultivating a love for purposeful labor and aligning our daily activities with our spiritual goals, we resist the allure of indolence and its consequential stagnation.

In addition to personal virtue cultivation, the sacraments of the Church play an indispensable role in overcoming vices. Sacraments are not mere rituals; they are encounters with divine grace that equip us to transcend our human weaknesses. Regular participation in the Eucharist fortifies the believer with Christ's presence, enabling a deeper communion with God and empowering a life oriented towards virtue.

Moreover, the sacrament of Reconciliation offers a continual means by which the faithful can address their failings and renew their commitment to a life free of vice. This sacrament not only forgives but also restores the grace needed to resist future temptations, encouraging a persistent striving toward holiness. It reminds us that falling is a part of the human journey, but with God's grace, so is rising.

The Church, as a community of believers, provides additional support in the pursuit of overcoming vices. In the fellowship of the Church, we find encouragement, accountability, and tangible expressions of God's love. Community acts as both a mirror and a guide; it reflects the areas where we need growth and offers guidance and inspiration through the witness of others.

Furthermore, sacred scripture serves as an instructional guide in this struggle against vice. The teachings of the Gospels and the epistles of the apostles provide profound insights into the human condition and offer practical encouragement for overcoming sin. Regular reflection and meditation on scripture arm the believer with wisdom and understanding, nurturing both mind and spirit.

Finally, prayer stands as the lifeline in this battle against vice. Through prayer, we develop a relationship with God, one that sustains and empowers us amid temptation. Prayer invites the Holy Spirit to work within us, transforming our hearts and enabling us to align more closely with divine will. It is through prayer that we seek the courage, strength, and virtue necessary to overcome the vices that entangle us.

In conclusion, the battle to overcome the seven vices is both a personal challenge and a spiritual mission. With the aid of divine grace, the cultivation of virtue, the support of the Church, and the power of prayer, this mission is achievable. It calls each individual not only to resist temptation but to actively pursue holiness, thereby reflecting the image of Christ more clearly in the world. This journey, though arduous, promises transformation, hope, and an everlasting union with the Creator.

Chapter 20: The Seven Sacraments

In the symphony of Catholic doctrine, the Seven Sacraments stand as pivotal notes, each contributing to a harmonious composition that echoes the divine rhythm of grace. These sacred rites—Baptism, Eucharist, Confirmation, Reconciliation, Anointing of the Sick, Holy Orders, and Matrimony—are outward symbols of inward grace, instituted by Christ as channels for spiritual nourishment and communal sanctification. More than mere rituals, they are profound encounters with the divine, inviting believers into a deeper union with God and the Church. As instruments of grace, the Sacraments play a vital role in the lifelong journey of faith, transforming the mundane into the miraculous and guiding souls toward eternal life. Through them, the faithful receive not only the assurance of God's presence but also the strength to live out the Gospel in a world that often forgets its Creator. Thus, understanding the Sacraments is essential for any Catholic apologist striving to articulate and defend the richness of the faith, as they are both a testament to God's unwavering love and a call to active participation in His divine plan.

Introduction to the Sacraments

The sacramental life of the Roman Catholic Church represents a meeting point between the divine and the earthly, a tangible manifestation of God's grace bestowed upon the faithful. The sacraments, instituted by Christ, serve as conduits of divine grace, enabling believers to partake in the divine life here and now. This sacred participation not only signifies a deeper communion with God but also reflects the Church's mission to sanctify humanity and the world.

In understanding the sacraments, one must first contemplate their essence. At the heart of Catholic theology, sacraments are not merely symbolic gestures or rites of passage. They are efficacious signs, meaning they effect what they signify. Through them, grace is not only represented; it is truly conferred upon the recipient. This notion elevates sacraments beyond mere human rituals to divinely instituted means of grace. As a result, they are both mysterious and accessible, simultaneously transcendent and immanent.

The sacraments can be seen as a bridge between what is visible and the invisible, between the material world and the spiritual realm. Each sacrament incorporates a material element—such as water in Baptism or bread and wine in the Eucharist—which becomes a vessel of spiritual reality. In this fusion of the physical and the spiritual, the sacraments invite believers to experience the mystical union of their earthly lives with the divine plan that transcends temporal existence.

Moreover, the role of the sacraments stretches into the foundational structure of Catholic ecclesiology, the study of the Church. They signify and realize a profound ecclesial communion. When a sacrament is celebrated, not only the individual recipient is fortified, but the entire Church is spiritually enriched. Thus, the sacraments foster unity among believers, drawing them into a shared faith experience, a communal life within the Body of Christ.

Historically, this understanding emerged out of centuries of theological reflection and development. Early Church Fathers articulated the basis of sacramental theology with profound insight, setting a foundation that theologians like Saint Augustine and Saint Thomas Aquinas would later expand into a comprehensive sacramental doctrine. Aquinas, for instance, saw sacraments as instruments of God's grace, indispensable for our spiritual journey towards salvation. These theological insights continue to guide the faithful in appreciating the profound depth of the Church's sacramental life.

Yet, the sacraments are not magical rites; they necessitate a proper disposition to bear fruit in the believer's life. This disposition involves faith, a humble openness to receive God's grace, and a commitment to live out the implications of receiving that grace. In this way, the sacraments not only mark important milestones in a Christian's spiritual journey but also challenge the faithful to grow continuously in holiness and virtue. They are dynamic, calling believers to transformation and renewal.

In grappling with the significance of sacraments, the Catholic apologist faces both an opportunity and a challenge. The mystery inherent in sacraments can become a subject of skepticism, particularly among those who question the efficacy of grace-sanctioned rituals. However, this same mystery can be a powerful testimony to the depth and richness of the Catholic faith. By presenting the sacraments as instances where divine grace meets human existence, apologists can articulate a compelling vision of a lived, grace-filled Catholic identity.

For theologians and believers alike, sacraments are not to be viewed in isolation but as interwoven into the broader tapestry of Catholic life and doctrine. Each sacrament holds its own unique graces and purpose, contributing to a holistic Christian witness. Baptism initiates one into the Christian community, the Eucharist nourishes the soul, Confession restores broken relationships with God, and so on. Together, they map out the spiritual journey from initiation through growth and service to the final embrace of eternal life.

In our present age, the sacraments offer a response to modern challenges by grounding believers in a tangible encounter with the divine amidst a world that often seems divested of spiritual meaning. In their celebration, ritual becomes a repository of time-tested wisdom and a haven of spiritual respite. They are thus essential in fostering both personal and communal holiness, guiding the faithful in their shared pilgrimage toward the ultimate fulfillment of God's promises.

The Seven Sacraments, therefore, are not just rites of the past or formalities of tradition. They stand at the core of Catholic life, emblematic of the perennial dialogue between God and humanity. Their enduring relevance challenges each generation to embrace them not merely as acts to be performed but as transformative encounters, as moments where heaven touches earth and transforms lives at the deepest level.

Baptism, Eucharist, and Confirmation

The sacraments are a cornerstone of Roman Catholic theology, each serving as a visible sign of the invisible grace conferred by God. Among these, Baptism, Eucharist, and Confirmation hold a foundational significance, not only in their individual effects on the soul but in their collective role in the life of a believer. They form the heart of Christian initiation, making believers part of the Church and strengthening their faith journey.

Baptism, often referred to as the "gateway" sacrament, is the first and fundamental sacrament of initiation. Its theological roots are deeply embedded in the teachings of the New Testament, particularly the Great Commission (Matthew 28:19), where Christ commands, "Go and make disciples of all nations, baptizing them in the name of the Father and of the Son and of the Holy Spirit." Baptism cleanses one of original sin and marks the beginning of the Christian life. Through the rite of water and the invocation of the Holy Trinity, the baptized are born anew, becoming part of the Communion of Saints and members of the Christian community.

Yet Baptism is not simply a rite of purification but an initiation into a communal life centered around Christ. It represents a profound transformation of identity, where the individual becomes a participant in the life, death, and resurrection of Jesus. This transformation is not merely symbolic—it's a realignment of the individual's existence towards the divine. The newly initiated take on the mantle of Christ, embracing a life marked by grace and a mission to embody the virtues of the Gospel.

The Eucharist is the pinnacle of Catholic life, referred to as the "source and summit" of Christian life by the Second Vatican Council. In the celebration of the Mass, the faithful are not only reminded of but made present to the sacrificial love of Christ. The doctrine of transubstantiation articulates the miraculous transformation of bread and wine into the actual body and blood of Jesus Christ. This mystery, respecting the limits of human reason, invites a profound act of faith. By partaking in the Eucharist, believers are united with Christ in an intimate and transformative communion, reinforcing their faith journey that began in Baptism.

In essence, the Eucharist serves as both a meal and a sacrifice. It recalls the Last Supper, where Christ instituted this sacrament and offered himself as the ultimate paschal sacrifice. This dual nature encapsulates the complexity and richness of Catholic theology—the Eucharist is a celebration of God's manifold grace and the continuation of Christ's salvific work in the world. Participating in it requires not only belief in its sacred reality but also a commitment to live out its implications in daily life.

Confirmation, often seen as the strengthening of what began in Baptism, seals the Christian with the gifts of the Holy Spirit. This sacrament is rich with imagery and tradition, often likened to the descent of the Holy Spirit upon the apostles at Pentecost. Through Confirmation, the faithful receive the grace to mature in their spiritual life and take up greater responsibilities within the Church and society. It is an empowerment for mission, emboldening believers to witness and defend their faith.

In this sacrament, there is an encounter with the Holy Spirit, who imparts seven gifts: wisdom, understanding, counsel, fortitude, knowledge, piety, and fear of the Lord. These gifts serve as spiritual tools, equipping the confirmed to confront the challenges of life and the temptations of the secular world. They act as fortification in a world where faith is continuously tested and scrutinized.

The significance of Baptism, Eucharist, and Confirmation cannot be overstated in the Catholic tradition. They do not merely mark stages of spiritual growth but actively contribute to the development of a lifelong bond with the Divine. Each sacrament involves participation in the communal and ecclesial life of the Church, establishing not only a relationship with God but also with fellow believers.

To fully grasp the importance of these sacraments, one must consider their interconnectedness in the life of Catholic doctrine. Baptism initiates the believer into the faith, the Eucharist nourishes and sustains, while Confirmation strengthens and commissions. Together, they form a solid foundation, enabling the faithful to live lives that reflect the love and teachings of Christ.

In sum, these sacraments address the human condition, offering healing and sanctification through divine grace. They invite believers into a sublime relationship with God, encouraging growth towards spiritual maturity and fostering unity with the Church. In Baptism, one finds rebirth; in the Eucharist, nourishment; and in Confirmation, empowerment. Thus, they are not simply rites of passage but ongoing encounters with God's love and mercy, echoing the perpetual call towards holiness and service to others.

Chapter 21: Reconciliation, Anointing of the Sick, and Holy Orders

As we journey deeper into the sacraments of healing and service, let's consider how Reconciliation, Anointing of the Sick, and Holy Orders embody the profound mystery of divine grace that operates within the church to sanctify, heal, and consecrate. Reconciliation, often called confession, manifests God's infinite mercy, inviting sinners back to communion with Him, a testament to the transformative power vested in the confessor's authority. The Anointing of the Sick extends grace and healing both spiritually and, at times, physically, to those suffering, symbolizing a tangible encounter with Christ's compassion and a strengthening of faith in the face of mortality. Holy Orders, on the other hand, binds men to a life of service and leadership in Christ's name, a profound dedication that ensures the perpetuation of Christ's mission on earth. Each sacrament distinctly reflects the interplay of human need and divine response, reminding us that in our frailty or vocation, there lies an intricate balance of justice, mercy, and divine calling that sustains the faithful. Together, these sacraments not only fortify individual believers but also combine the communal livelihood of the faithful, underscoring the Catholic Church's mission to seek, heal, and serve.

Deep Dive into Healing and Service Sacraments

In the Catholic tradition, the sacraments of Reconciliation, Anointing of the Sick, and Holy Orders are profound mysteries of faith which offer grace in distinct yet interconnected ways. These sacraments serve the dual purpose of individual sanctification and service to the broader ecclesial community. For Roman Catholics, understanding these sacraments is not just about knowledge, but about embracing a lived reality that reflects the core of Christian discipleship and divine mercy.

Reconciliation, colloquially known as Confession, is a sacrament of healing that provides spiritual restoration. At its heart is the belief in the boundless mercy of God—a God who actively seeks to reconcile humankind and restore harmony to wounded souls tarnished by sin. This sacrament emphasizes the infinite capability for healing, underscoring that neither individual nor communal sin is beyond God's redemption. It invites a theological reflection on sin itself, the nature of human fallibility, and the ever-present grace that seeks to restore the ruptured relationship between the Creator and the created.

This sacrament also elevates the penitent's journey toward spiritual wholeness through contrition, confession, and satisfaction. These steps are not mere rituals; they are transformative encounters where the believer acknowledges personal shortcomings while inviting Christ's mercy into their heart. The reconciliatory process compels one to face their failures with honesty and humility—a humbling yet liberating experience that underscores the essential Christian message of forgiveness and renewal.

Anointing of the Sick, however, shifts focus slightly from spiritual to holistic healing. While it is often misconceived as last rites intended solely for those at life's end, the sacrament is more accurately understood as a channel of God's grace during times of illness. It recognizes the physical and emotional toll of suffering and invites the divine into the human plight, fostering a sense of hope and serenity amidst turmoil. This sacrament is performed with the laying on of hands and anointing with oil, symbolizing strength and fortitude endowed by the Holy Spirit.

The theological import of Anointing of the Sick lies in its affirmation of life, even in the face of death. It is a testimony to the intrinsic worth of every person, affirming that their dignity does not diminish with health challenges. Through this sacrament, the Church acts as a conduit of divine compassion, emphasizing solidarity with those who suffer. The sacrament is a clarion call to care for one another, reminding the Church of its mission to be an ever-present source of solace and encouragement for the ailing.

In this sacramental economy, Holy Orders is particularly unique. It is a sacrament dedicated to service and vocation, perpetuating the mission of Christ through the ordained ministry. It forms the backbone of Church leadership, encompassing the roles of deacons, priests, and bishops, each contributing distinctively to the ecclesiastical framework. The sacrament of Holy Orders epitomizes Christ's servant leadership, challenging those

ordained to embody humility, sacrifice, and unwavering commitment to the faith
community.

The theological depth of Holy Orders underscores the transformative power of vocation,
where the individual is consecrated for a life wholly aligned to God's work. This sacrament
reinforces the communal nature of faith, where ordained ministers serve as the hands and
voice of Christ in pastoral duties and sacramental administration. Through Holy Orders, the
Church ensures a continual apostolic succession, maintaining an unbroken lineage of
service and ecclesial leadership throughout centuries.

To grasp the essence of these sacraments requires a shift from looking at them as mere
rites to perceiving them as living embodiments of Christ's love and grace. They engage both
the individual and the community in a profound dialogue with the divine, offering healing,
hope, and a deeper spiritual commitment. Each sacrament, whether healing or service-
oriented, fortifies the believer's journey toward holiness, fostering a deeper unity with God
and others.

The intersection of Reconciliation, Anointing of the Sick, and Holy Orders reveals much
about the Church's understanding of human experience and divine intervention. They
invite skepticism to dissolve into wonder, transforming doubt into an opportunity for
deeper understanding. By engaging with these sacraments, one embarks on a path of
transformative faith, where divine mystery and human vulnerability meet in the sacred
space of trust, grace, and redemption.

In conclusion, these sacraments present themselves not merely as theological concepts but
as active engagements with God. They call for a renewed understanding from scholars and
skeptics alike, encouraging all to contemplate their roles in personal and communal
growth. Ultimately, they stand as testaments to a faith that is continually being realized and
expressed, inviting everyone into a profound relationship with the divine.

Chapter 22: Matrimony

Matrimony, in the Roman Catholic vision, illuminates the profound mystery of divine love and human communion. Marriage is far more than a mere social contract; it embodies a sacred covenant reflecting Christ's unwavering bond with His Church. Within this sacrament, two individual journeys meld into one pilgrimage, blessed by God's grace, orienting them towards holiness and mutual salvation. Theologians have long marveled at how marriage mirrors the Creator's love: creative, unwavering, and life-giving. Through the selfless exchange of vows, husband and wife become co-creators with God, tasked with nurturing life and faith within their domestic church—the family. Guided by the Holy Spirit, this union calls Catholics to a higher standard of love marked by fidelity, sacrifice, and enduring commitment. It's a lifelong commitment that reinforces the virtues of patience, understanding, and charity, serving as a wellspring of spiritual growth and communal strength. Herein lies not just a personal journey but a profound participation in the Church's mission, inviting skeptics and believers alike to witness the transforming power of God's love made manifest in the sacrament.

Theology of Marriage

The sacrament of Matrimony, in the Roman Catholic tradition, represents not just a legal bond but a profound theological reality. At its core, the Theology of Marriage acknowledges the divine institution of marriage as an integral part of creation's order. When God created mankind, He inscribed within human nature the vocation to love, a call inherently fulfilled in the marital covenant. Such is the foundation upon which Catholic doctrine rests in understanding marriage – not as a mere social contract but a sacred covenant between a man, a woman, and God.

The conjugal bond is emblematic of Christ's unfaltering love for the Church. This mystery is illuminated in the writings of Saint Paul, who, in his epistle to the Ephesians, draws a parallel between the relationship of Christ and the Church and the unity of husband and wife. This allegory serves to elevate marriage to a supernatural dimension, imbued with the grace to reflect divine love. It is a mutual gift of self, a living sign of God's presence in the world.

The encyclical "Humanae Vitae," authored by Pope Paul VI, articulates the inseparability of the unitive and procreative dimensions of marriage. In this teaching, the Roman Catholic Church affirms that the marital act is not solely for mutual love and support but also inherently open to the transmission of life. This dual aspect highlights the uniqueness of matrimonial love, which imitates the creative power of God Himself.

Marriage, according to Catholic faith, is not immune to the trials inherent in human existence. The entrance into this sacrament is a commitment made in the presence of the Church community, reflecting the public nature of the covenant. The vows of fidelity, openness to procreation, and indissolubility articulate the demands of this sacred union. In a world often beset by the transient nature of relationships, these vows stand as a bulwark against the waves of moral relativism.

Indissolubility is perhaps the most challenging tenet for contemporary audiences to grasp. Yet, it's here we find a profound truth about the divine plan – marriage is intended to be a permanent institution. This permanence reflects God's unwavering commitment to mankind. It's an assurance that through every joy and struggle, the marital bond remains an enduring testament to steadfast love. It's crucial to understand that indissolubility is not just an arbitrary rule but a divine safeguard designed to protect the sanctity of family life.

The theology of marriage also emphasizes the importance of the family as the "domestic church." Within the sanctuary of the home, parents become primary educators in faith, nurturing their children in the ways of virtue and holiness. This 'ecclesiola' mirrors the larger Church and plays a crucial role in transmitting the faith across generations. Thus, the vitality of the Church is inherently linked to the health of marriages and families within her bosom.

Furthermore, the sacrament of Matrimony exemplifies the call to holiness through the daily acts of love and sacrifice inherent in married life. It's a training ground for virtues –

patience, humility, charity – that prepare couples for their ultimate union with God. Through the trials of marriage, couples learn the art of forgiveness, mirroring the infinite mercy of God.

In conclusion, understanding the Theology of Marriage within the Catholic context requires a comprehensive appreciation of its sacred nature and divine purpose. It invites us to see beyond the temporal aspects and grasp the eternal significance of a bond forged in love and sustained by grace. The sacrament is both a gift and a mission, calling married couples to witness to the world the mystery of God's enduring love through their faithful and fruitful union.

Thus, in a society that often undervalues the sacrament's profundity, the task of Catholic apologetics is to articulate and defend these truths — inspiring not just belief but a lived experience of this divine vocation. The apostolic mission of the Church, then, is not merely to maintain doctrines but to serve as a luminous beacon illuminating the beauty and sanctity of Christian marriage for a world in search of authentic love.

Practical Guide to a Catholic Marriage

Matrimony, elevated to a sacrament by Christ, invites us into a profound mystery where the earthly intersects the divine. This union is not merely a legal or social contract but a sacred covenant, reflecting the unbreakable bond between Christ and His Church. To truly grasp the nature of Catholic marriage, one must first understand its theological foundation—the perpetual, sacrificial love that mirrors the love of God for humanity.

At the heart of Catholic marriage lies the commitment to permanence. The Church teaches that marriage is a lifelong partnership, an "until death do us part" vow that demands not only love but fidelity, sacrifice, and mutual support. This permanence is not a burden but a blessing. It offers stability and a sense of security, allowing both partners to grow in love and holiness. The promise to stay together through sickness, health, riches, and poverty is more than words; it's a testament to faith and the real grace of the sacrament.

For those contemplating matrimony, a deep understanding of the sacrament's significance is vital. In preparation, couples must engage in pre-marital counseling, which often includes sessions with a priest or certified Church counselor. These sessions explore various aspects of married life, covering everything from financial responsibility to spiritual growth. Emphasis is placed on learning effective communication, understanding each other's roles, and developing a shared vision for the future—all essential tools for a thriving marriage.

Communication, arguably, is the bedrock of any lasting relationship. The ability to listen and speak with love, respect, and honesty cannot be overstated. Catholic couples are encouraged to cultivate practices that enhance dialogue and understanding. Daily prayers, shared worship experiences, and regular couple retreats offer opportunities to deepen the spiritual and emotional bond. Moreover, maintaining transparency in all areas of life—from finances to family planning—fosters mutual trust and respect.

Within a marriage, love should be a living, dynamic force. The Church calls spouses to love one another as Christ loves the Church—with selflessness and humility. This love is expressed not only in grand gestures but in everyday acts of kindness, patience, and consideration. It's about putting the other's needs before one's own, forgiving readily, and supporting each other in times of trial and triumph.

Financial stewardship also forms a crucial element of Catholic matrimony. Married couples are advised to view their material resources as gifts entrusted to them by God, meant for the benefit of the family and the broader community. Practicing good stewardship requires open discussions about finances, setting shared goals, and living simply to allow for generosity towards others—both family and the less fortunate. Importantly, avoiding the pitfalls of materialism calls for a conscious balance between necessity and excess.

Another cornerstone of Catholic marriage is the openness to life. The Church teaches that one of the primary ends of marriage is the procreation and education of children. However, this openness is about more than just physical reproduction; it's about nurturing a welcoming spirit. Whether a couple is blessed with children or not, the call is to nurture life's values in all aspects, fostering a family that is a domestic church—a beacon of faith and love in the larger community.

When challenges arise, and they inevitably will, the Catholic couple can find solace in the sacramental grace of matrimony. This grace does not immunize against suffering but provides the strength and courage to face hardships together. The Church's rich traditions, such as the sacraments of Eucharist and Reconciliation, offer spouses the spiritual sustenance needed to navigate life's vicissitudes.

The sanctification of marriage is a continuous journey, requiring a willing heart and a faithful spirit. Participation in Church life, involvement in parish activities, and commitment to the faith community are both supportive and transformational. As marriage counselors often advise, a couple's spiritual life should not be relegated to four walls of a church; it's a lived reality, reflected in every action, choice, and interaction.

In conclusion, the practical guidance for a Catholic marriage rests on living out its deep spiritual truths daily. It's a call to live sacrificially, love unconditionally, and grow in holiness together—the beautiful dance of two becoming one in Christ. Through this sacred covenant, Catholic couples contribute not only to each other's sanctity but also to a world hungry for witnesses of genuine, enduring love.

Chapter 23: The Seven Dogmas of Catholicism

The Seven Dogmas of Catholicism stand as the foundational bedrock upon which the faith's truths are firmly established and proclaimed. These dogmas act not merely as decrees of belief but, rather, as illuminating truths that guide the intellect and heart towards greater understanding and communion with the divine. They encompass the profound mysteries of faith, including the doctrines of the Trinity and the Incarnation, which reveal God's unfathomable nature and His intimate participation in human history. The dogmas concerning the Immaculate Conception and the Assumption of Mary elevate the dignity of human cooperation in salvation. Meanwhile, teachings on the authority of the papacy anchor the Church's continuity and unity. Each dogma, in its unique way, articulates the inexhaustible richness of the Catholic faith, calling scholars, theologians, and skeptics to delve more deeply into the mysteries that sustain faith and cultivate the soul's ascent towards truth. Recognizing these dogmas not as limitations but as gateways to divine wisdom allows for a more profound engagement with the enduring questions of human existence and God's eternal love.

Overview of Catholic Dogmas

The fabric of Catholicism is rich with truths that span centuries, encapsulating beliefs that define the faith's identity. Among these lies the cornerstone: dogma. Catholic dogmas are not merely a series of abstract declarations; they are living truths that resonate through time, embodying the Church's unyielding commitment to divine revelation. This exploration of Catholic dogmas seeks to illuminate how these foundational truths guide the faithful, anchoring them firmly to the teachings of Christ and His Church.

Dogmas in Catholicism serve a crucial role. They act as definitive truths that every Catholic is called to believe. Unlike theological opinions or speculative theology, dogmas are immutable truths that have been solemnly defined by the Church's Magisterium. The essence of dogma is thus rooted in infallibility; it is believed to be divinely revealed and irrevocable. Here, the Church acts not as an innovator but as a custodian of the truth handed down through Divine Revelation, Sacred Scripture, and Sacred Tradition.

One might wonder why such dogmas are necessary. The need for dogma finds its rationale in the very nature of human inquiry and the reality of revelation. Humans are seekers of truth, and in the vast expanses of spiritual exploration, dogma offers a compass. It is not restrictive but liberating, allowing a more profound union with the faith while providing clarity. Dogmas articulate what has always been believed universally by the faithful, serving as a testament to the unity and continuity within the Church.

The process through which dogmas are defined is meticulous and sacred. The Church, guided by the Holy Spirit, engages in deep theological reflection before formal declarations. This often occurs in response to misunderstandings or heresies that arise, aiming to clarify the faith for the benefit of all believers. Ecumenical Councils, such as Nicaea and Trent, have historically been pivotal in formally defining and defending dogmas, combating heresies that sought to distort essential truths.

The significance of dogmas extends beyond mere doctrinal affirmation; it shapes the lived experience of Catholics. The truths encapsulated in dogmas influence moral teachings, liturgical practices, and daily devotion. By grounding their lives in these truths, the faithful are equipped to engage with the world through a lens of faith that is robust and unshakeable. In this context, dogmas are not just intellectual assent but calls to embrace a way of life aligned with divine will.

In pondering the intricate nature of Catholic dogmas, their evolution and reception also come under consideration. There exists a dynamic relationship between dogma and doctrine, the latter of which can develop and expand in understanding over time. This development does not imply a change in truth but rather a deepening comprehension. The Church, therefore, does not create new dogmas in response to contemporary issues but instead draws upon the timeless truths revealed through Christ.

Throughout history, challenges to dogma have arisen from within and outside the Church. These challenges have often prompted significant theological reflection and reaffirmation of core truths. Heresies, such as Arianism and Pelagianism, once threatened to undermine the foundational beliefs of Christianity, but it was through the articulation and defense of dogma that the Church remained steadfast. Modern challenges to dogma often come in the form of relativism and secularism, urging a continual engagement with the world while remaining anchored in truth.

Moreover, dogma's influence extends into the realm of ecumenism and interfaith dialogue. While dogmas are inherently particular to Catholicism, they also serve as a starting point for understanding and collaboration with other Christian denominations and world religions. By articulating the unchanging truths of the faith, dogmas invite others into dialogue, fostering mutual understanding while maintaining doctrinal purity.

It is essential to remember that at the heart of dogma lies a profound mystery – the mystery of God as revealed in Jesus Christ. The articulation of dogma, therefore, calls the faithful to a deeper relationship with this mystery, inviting contemplation and awe. At the same time, the certainty of dogma offers consolation in a world where truth is often seen as subjective and elusive.

In conclusion, the overview of Catholic dogmas provides a lens through which the faithful can view the timeless truths of their faith. These dogmas, solemnly defined and perpetually united across time, constitute the very essence of Catholic teaching. For apologists, theologians, and scholars, understanding and articulating these dogmas is crucial in defending the faith and guiding others into the profound mysteries of God's revelation. As the Church navigates the complexities of the modern world, it remains unwavering, buoyed by the truths that dogma safeguards, ever committed to the mission entrusted to it by Christ Himself.

Key Dogmatic Teachings

To embark on understanding the key dogmatic teachings of the Catholic Church, one must first grasp the profundity and depth that the Church has maintained throughout centuries. These teachings are not mere doctrines; they are the lifeblood that has perpetuated the faith, a gift given through divine revelation, ecclesiastical authority, and human pursuit of truth. At the core of these teachings lies a commitment to truth as revealed by God through Jesus Christ, a commitment which the Church believes is unchanging and universal.

The notion of dogma in Catholicism serves as a pillar that upholds the structure of the faith. It is essential to recognize the role of dogma as both a protective boundary for faith and an invitation to explore the mysteries of divine revelation more deeply. Catholic dogma presents itself not as a restriction but as a guide—a map that points towards the ultimate truth while ensuring the fidelity to the same truth that Christ imparted.

Foremost among these dogmas is the mystery of the Holy Trinity—Father, Son, and Holy Spirit—three persons in one God. This is not simply a conceptual puzzle but the very essence of Christian belief. The Trinity reflects the eternal relationship and communal love within the Godhead, a divine relationality that informs how Catholics perceive relationships in creation. The language around the Trinity often borrows from philosophical thought, yet its roots are squarely planted in the scriptural revelation that Christians cherish and seek to understand more fully.

Closely following this dogmatic core is the Incarnation. The belief that Jesus Christ is both fully divine and fully human forms the heart of Christianity. This teaching highlights the intimacy between God and humanity, revealing a God who steps into the very fabric of human existence, suffering, and joy by becoming man. The Incarnation challenges believers to see the divine in the mundane, to find God in the messiness and beauty of life.

The concept of original sin and the necessity of grace continues the Church's central teachings. The doctrine of original sin speaks to the fractured nature of the world and humanity, portraying a world in need of redemption. Yet, in the teaching of grace, the Church presents the remedy—a path to restoration and wholeness through God's freely given love. This theme permeates the sacraments and practices of the Church as channels of grace that invite believers to partake in divine life.

In addition to these profound mysteries, the dogmatic teachings on the Resurrection and Ascension of Christ declare hope and promise. The Resurrection affirms life over death, assuring believers that death doesn't have the final word. It speaks to the eternal destiny of all creation and emphasizes the transformational power of God's love. The Ascension similarly clarifies that Christ's physical absence doesn't signify abandonment but an enduring presence through the Holy Spirit and the Church.

The Immaculate Conception and Assumption of Mary, although often misunderstood, echo the Church's honor for the Mother of God. These dogmas emphasize the unique role of Mary in salvation history and her exemplary discipleship. The Immaculate Conception affirms that from her very beginning, Mary was preserved from original sin, preparing her to be the Mother of the Savior. The Assumption, celebrated for its depiction of the fulfillment of redemption, depicts Mary's participation in her Son's resurrection, and serves as a powerful symbol of hope for all believers.

Finally, the dogma of papal infallibility emerges as a critical tenet in the Church's understanding of authority and spiritual guidance. Declared relatively recently in the annals of Church history, it asserts the Pope's authority to proclaim certain doctrines of faith and morals free from error. This ensures a continuity and safeguard for essential truths, providing the faithful with a reliable source of doctrinal clarity amidst the turmoil of theological and cultural shifts.

While other belief systems may prioritize experience or scripture alone, Catholic dogma pulls together the rich traditions, sacred texts, and authoritative teachings to form a robust framework for understanding God and living the faith. Each dogma encourages reasoned contemplation and debate, ensuring a living and dynamic faith rather than a stagnant one.

It's important to challenge misconceptions about dogma as being rigid or anachronistic. These profound teachings, when approached with an earnest heart and open mind, resonate with the timeless quest of humanity to connect deeply with the transcendent and understand our place within the cosmos. In this pursuit, dogmatic teachings awaken the conscience, inspire the will, and sustain the faithful journey of every believer.

Catholicism invites all to ponder these truths, to discuss and deliberate them, and most importantly, to live by them. The intellectual and spiritual engagement with these teachings invokes a harmony between faith and reason, encouraging believers not simply to adopt these truths passively, but to internalize and express them through the daily course of life.

Thus, through the lens of dogma, the Catholic Church not only preserves the essence of Christ's message but also invites every seeker of truth to embark on a transformative journey. This journey, with all its intellectual rigor and spiritual depth, is both personal and communal—a testament to the universal call of Catholic existence to love God and neighbor in ever-deepening faith, hope, and charity.

Chapter 24: Articulating the Faith

In the landscape of modern dialogue, effectively conveying the essence of the Roman Catholic faith demands a delicate blend of clarity, compassion, and conviction. Articulating the faith isn't merely about presenting doctrinal truths; it's about fostering an understanding that resonates with both heart and mind, inviting skeptics and seekers into a transformative journey. Our communication strategies must be tailored to bridge perceived chasms between the Church's teachings and today's existential questions. As we grapple with secular thought and diverse perspectives, the challenge lies in presenting the timeless wisdom of the Church in a way that is both intellectually rigorous and personally compelling. Engaging in authentic dialogue requires patience and skill, encouraging open questions while steadfastly sharing the profound beauty of Catholic truth. In this chapter, we navigate the pathways of discourse that not only defend but also reveal the faith's depth, lighting a path towards conversion and renewal for those who seek genuine understanding.

Effective Communication Strategies

Articulating the faith is an endeavor delicate yet profoundly significant. Effective communication strategies are indispensable for apologists seeking to engage with others about the complexities and beauties of the Roman Catholic faith. The heart of effective communication lies in understanding both the content to be conveyed and the audience to whom it is presented. Without this dual awareness, the message may falter, entangled in misunderstanding or misinterpretation.

To begin with, clarity is the cornerstone of effective communication. The teachings and principles of the Catholic Church, though immensely rich, can also be intricate. As communicators of the faith, Roman Catholic scholars and theologians must strive for expression that is clear and comprehensible, avoiding unnecessary jargon or overly technical language that might alienate or confuse the listener. Simplicity doesn't necessarily mean surface-level engagement; rather, it's the ability to distill complex theological and philosophical truths into accessible ideas that resonate with both the initiated and the seeker alike.

Another pivotal aspect is empathy. The communicator should endeavor to understand the listener's perspective—whether they be a fellow believer, a skeptic, or a seeker. Genuine listening creates an atmosphere of respect and openness, setting a fertile ground for meaningful dialogue. Empathy bridges the gap between differing worldviews and fosters an environment where difficult questions can be addressed compassionately and sincerely.

In tandem with empathy, respect is also crucial. Every individual holds unique beliefs and experiences that shape their understanding of the world. Engaging others with respect demonstrates the apologist's recognition of their inherent dignity, echoing the Church's teachings on human dignity. Respect also involves acknowledging valid doubts and questions, which can pave the way for a constructive exchange of ideas.

Beyond empathy and respect, there's a need for adaptability. Communication is not a one-size-fits-all endeavor. Effective communicators adapt their approach based on their audience's background, needs, and expectations. This might mean altering the method of delivery or rephrasing the message without compromising its truth. An apologist should be ready to switch from scholarly discourse to personal anecdotes or from philosophical arguments to practical examples, depending on what's most suitable for the audience.

The art of questioning cannot be understated in its importance. Thoughtful questions stimulate curiosity, invite participation, and encourage deeper reflection on the truths of faith. Questions should prompt rather than coerce, encouraging a journey of discovery rather than imposing a rigid path. By asking open-ended questions, apologists can gently guide others to explore their beliefs, assumptions, and the teachings of the Church.

Moreover, effective communication requires a balance between conviction and humility. While it is essential to be firm in one's beliefs, it is equally vital to remain open to dialogue and further learning. Humility allows the communicator to admit when they don't have all the answers and to remain receptive to insights from others. This openness not only enriches the communicator's understanding but also models a posture of learning that others may mirror.

In our interdependent world influenced by digital advancements, leveraging technology responsibly can amplify the reach and impact of the Catholic message. Utilizing digital platforms like blogs, podcasts, and social media can open up vast opportunities to share the faith with a global audience. However, the digital realm also demands discernment and intentionality. It requires the communicator to remain authentic and grounded in truth while engaging with varied and often fleeting online interactions.

Storytelling is another powerful strategy. Human beings are inherently drawn to stories, which have the ability to convey truth in a manner that resonates on a personal and emotional level. Sharing narratives from sacred scripture, Church history, or personal testimonies can illuminate aspects of the faith in a way abstract reasoning or doctrinal teaching might not. Stories capture attention, convey emotion, and illustrate how faith plays out in the lived experience of individuals and communities.

Furthermore, patience is a vital virtue in the context of effective communication. Hearts and minds are rarely changed in an instant. The journey from skepticism to faith, or even from doubt to contemplation, takes time. Patience involves recognizing that sowing seeds of belief might not yield immediate fruit but trusting that they might germinate in time. This enduring patience should be coupled with persistent prayer, trusting in the Holy Spirit's work in the hearts of all engaged in dialogue.

Lastly, authenticity is indispensable. The most compelling witness to the faith is one that radiates genuine conviction and lived-out truth. It's about letting one's life be an example of the Catholic values one espouses. Authenticity builds trust and credibility, creating a more open and engaging platform for sharing deeper truths. When words align with actions, the message becomes not just heard but seen and felt, making a lasting impression.

In conclusion, effective communication strategies in articulating the faith involve a harmonious blend of clarity, empathy, respect, adaptability, questioning, conviction, and humility. Combining these with modern technological tools, storytelling, patience, and authenticity, Roman Catholic scholars and apologists are better equipped to engage honestly and thoughtfully in the profound mission of sharing and defending the faith. Through these efforts, the Catholic message can reach across boundaries and touch the lives of believers and seekers alike.

Engaging Skeptics and Seekers

Engaging both skeptics and seekers requires a nuanced approach, one that is built on understanding, empathy, and patience. It must acknowledge the diverse starting points from which individuals approach the topic of faith. Skeptics often have deeply rooted questions or experiences that have led them to harbor doubts. On the other hand, seekers may be open to faith but are cautious, feeling their way through the winding paths of spirituality with an earnest curiosity.

First, it's crucial to delineate the difference between skepticism and an active search for faith. Skeptics may often operate from a stance of intellectual or experiential resistance, while seekers might be more receptive, driven by a desire for belonging or existential understanding. Despite these differences, both groups are united by a genuine quest for truth. That quest deserves to be met with respect and an open dialogue rather than dogmatic assertions.

One must commence this engagement with an appreciation of the role doubt plays in an individual's faith journey. Doubt is not the enemy, but often the precursor to deeper understanding and commitment. Acknowledging doubt doesn't weaken the message but rather strengthens it by demonstrating faith's resilience and capacity to withstand scrutiny. It is the responsibility of Catholic apologists to welcome doubts as opportunities for meaningful discussion and reflection.

To begin addressing skeptics, it's necessary to display a profound commitment to intellectual honesty. This means not shying away from difficult questions or historical critiques. Skeptics are often most satisfied by responses that respect their intelligence and do not dismiss their inquiries. Thus, having a comprehensive understanding of Catholic teaching and its historical context is crucial. A well-founded explanation of Catholic doctrines and their development over time can illuminate the harmony between faith and reason.

Engagement with seekers requires a slightly different approach, emphasizing the Catholic faith's capacity to fulfill human longing for purpose and community. Seekers often look for narratives that resonate with their personal experiences. By demonstrating how Catholic teachings align with the core human desires for love, truth, and meaning, apologists can invite seekers into a journey that transcends mere intellectual acceptance to a holistic, lived faith.

In dealing with both groups, the authenticity of the apologist is key. Individuals engaged in spreading the faith must themselves embody the principles they espouse. Hypocrisy or double standards will only alienate those who are already cautious about religion's promises. Therefore, personal witness—living the virtues consistently and joyously—is one of the most potent tools of engagement.

Let us not forget the power of storytelling in this grand dialogue. The tradition of the Church is rich with narratives that illustrate faith in action, the power of conversion, and the grace found in communal ecclesiastical life. Stories of saints, historical movements within the Church, or modern examples of lived faith can provide tangible manifestations of abstract principles, making them more relatable and inspiring.

An effective engagement must also be dialogical, allowing for a two-way exchange. A genuine conversation respects the views and experiences of skeptics and seekers, enabling them to voice their concerns freely without fear of condemnation. This atmosphere of trust can catalyze a transformation, turning skepticism into curiosity and seeking into finding.

Additionally, technology must not be overlooked as an invaluable tool for engagement. Digital platforms have opened unprecedented opportunities for reaching a broader audience. Utilizing social media, podcasts, and online forums, Catholics can join conversations that were previously inaccessible, offering insights and forming communities in virtual spaces where today's skeptics and seekers often reside.

However, in all these efforts, the ultimate goal remains clear: leading individuals to a personal encounter with Jesus Christ. Apologists, by fortifying themselves with knowledge and genuine concern for others' spiritual well-being, can guide skeptics and seekers along paths that lead to this transformative encounter. In doing so, they help build a Church that is not only intellectual but also compassionate, welcoming, and profoundly true to its mission.

Chapter 25: Defending the Faith

The endeavor of defending the Roman Catholic faith demands both intellectual rigor and heartfelt devotion, as we engage with the questions and objections posed from a variety of perspectives. To respond effectively, we must approach each challenge with a blend of philosophical insight, scriptural understanding, and moral clarity. The key is not merely to refute arguments but to illuminate the truth and beauty of the faith, inviting the skeptic into a transformative dialogue. By mastering the art of apologetics, we strengthen our own beliefs while also providing a solid foundation for others who seek answers. This chapter navigates common objections, offering strategies and insights rooted in centuries of theological reflection, yet ever mindful of the evolving cultural context. It's through this robust engagement that the faith is not only defended but also understood more profoundly, drawing others toward the light of truth that the Church has safeguarded throughout the ages.

Responding to Common Objections

In the realm of defending the faith, facing objections is both an inevitable challenge and a vital opportunity. Objections should not be met with hostility, but rather as invitations to dialogue. The Roman Catholic Church, rich with centuries of theology and philosophical discourse, provides profound insights to address these objections, which often stem from misunderstandings or misconceptions. It's essential to approach these challenges not only with knowledge but also with a sense of charity and empathy.

One frequent objection centers around the perceived conflict between faith and reason. Critics argue that faith requires a suspension of rational thought, reducing religious belief to mere superstition. However, Catholic theology has long held that faith and reason are complementary rather than contradictory. The Church teaches that reason provides a foundation upon which faith is built, allowing believers to explore truths about existence and the divine. Using the works of thinkers like St. Thomas Aquinas, we can demonstrate how faith enriches and elevates reason, leading to a fuller understanding of the universe and our place within it.

Another common objection involves the role of the Church's authority. Skeptics often see the hierarchy and teachings of the Church as oppressive or outdated. They question the Church's moral and doctrinal authority, especially in light of modern secular values. Yet, historical analysis shows that the Church's authority has been a source of ethical guidance and stability throughout turbulent periods. It's important to explain how the Church's teachings are rooted in centuries of contemplation and a commitment to the common good, transcending the ephemeral nature of contemporary trends.

The problem of evil poses a significant challenge, as many struggle with reconciling the existence of a benevolent God with the presence of suffering in the world. This objection goes to the core of theodicy and requires a nuanced approach. Within Catholicism, suffering is not seen as a counterargument to God's goodness, but rather as an invitation to dig deeper into the mystery of suffering and redemption. The Passion of Christ is central to this exploration, illustrating how through suffering, redemption and resurrection are achieved. The Church views suffering as a potential path to spiritual growth and an opportunity for profound solidarity with others, particularly the poor and vulnerable.

Many objections also arise from historical misconceptions. Some claim that historical actions taken by the Church tarnish its moral authority. It's important to engage with these criticisms honestly, recognizing the imperfections within the Church's human history while also highlighting the immense good it has fostered. Acknowledging past mistakes allows the Church to demonstrate its commitment to truth and repentance. The lives of saints and the Church's vast contributions to education, healthcare, and social justice serve as powerful counter-narratives to these historical objections.

The accusation that the Catholic Church is closed-minded or resistant to scientific progress is another prevalent objection. History and modern scholarship both show that the Church has played a significant role in the advancement of science. Many clergy were, and still are, prominent scientists. The Church supports the idea that the study of the natural world can lead to a greater appreciation of God's creation. The Vatican Observatory and the Pontifical Academy of Sciences are contemporary examples of the Church's commitment to scientific inquiry.

Ethical objections often focus on the Church's teachings on issues like sexuality, contraception, and bioethics, which are perceived as restrictive or regressive. It is crucial to articulate that Catholic moral teachings are deeply rooted in the concept of natural law, affirming human dignity and the sanctity of life. These teachings are not arbitrary restrictions but rather guidelines aimed at respecting the natural order and promoting true human flourishing. Engaging skeptics requires not only explanation but also a demonstration of how these principles lead to a deeper sense of fulfillment and joy.

The relationship between Scripture and tradition can also raise objections. Critics argue that relying on tradition undermines the authority of the Bible. In defense, Catholic teaching emphasizes that Scripture and tradition are not in opposition but are part of a single deposit of faith. Tradition provides the context through which Scripture has been understood and lived out over the centuries. This living tradition helps ensure that interpretation remains faithful to the teachings of Christ and the apostles.

Addressing each of these objections provides not only an opportunity for clarification but also a deeper engagement with the heart of the faith we profess. Defending Catholicism necessitates a balance between reasoned argumentation and heartfelt witness. By embracing this approach, Catholic apologists can help others see the vibrancy and coherence of the faith, encouraging an authentic exploration of Catholic teachings and a genuine encounter with the divine. Through patient dialogue and a robust presentation of the faith, misunderstandings can be dispelled, leading to a greater understanding and appreciation of the Catholic tradition.

Strengthening Faith Through Apologetics

Apologetics, the art of defending the faith, serves as both a shield and a beacon for believers navigating the tumultuous waters of doubt and skepticism. For the Roman Catholic scholar, theologian, or even the skeptic in a journey towards conversion, understanding the value of apologetics is crucial. In a world increasingly driven by relativism and subjectivism, the ability to articulate one's beliefs with clarity and confidence becomes paramount.

The process of strengthening faith through apologetics begins with a commitment to understanding the Catholic faith's foundational teachings deeply. It demands more than a superficial acquaintance with doctrines; it calls for an intimate relationship with the tenets of faith that shape and define what it means to be Catholic. Through study and prayer, the apologist deepens their own faith, thus equipping themselves to explain and defend these truths to others.

One must consider how apologetics is not merely a defense mechanism but a proactive way to engage with others about the truths of Catholicism. By methodically and empathetically addressing the questions and objections of skeptics, apologists invite both themselves and others into a deeper understanding. This reciprocal nature of learning, teaching, and defending enriches the faith of all involved and helps build a community rooted in truth and love.

Additionally, apologetics encourages a reflective faith that seeks understanding (fides quaerens intellectum). Engaging with apologetic discourse pushes Catholics to scrutinize their own beliefs, stripping away unexamined assumptions and reinforcing a living, dynamic faith. It transforms belief into a conscious act of will, nurtured by reason and experience. As believers roam this reflective landscape, they begin to embody a faith that is not only personal but resonates universally.

The power of reason is a central pillar in the apologetic tradition. Far from diminishing the mystery and wonder of faith, reason enhances it by providing logical pathways that lead to spiritual truths. Respect for reason underscores the Church's belief in the harmony between faith and articulate rational discourse. Philosopher-theologians have long argued, using natural law and metaphysical principles, to demonstrate that faith and reason are not antithetical but complementary.

Historically, apologists have upheld this balance, providing rational explanations for the Church's teachings. By appealing to the intellect and the heart, apologetics respects the whole person, nurturing both the emotional and rational dimensions of faith. This holistic approach champions a faith that doesn't retreat from the world into blind adherence but engages it intellectually and spiritually. As such, apologists bear witness to a faith that is robust, meaningful, and deeply intertwined with the fabric of daily life.

Moreover, the role of apologetics extends beyond defense to become a tool for evangelization. By addressing contemporary challenges and questions, apologists act as bridges between the Church and the modern world. They translate the timeless truths of

Catholicism into accessible language, opening the door for meaningful dialogue. Through patience, empathy, and respect, they inspire others to explore the faith, potentially awakening a hunger for spiritual truths in those previously indifferent or hostile to the gospel message.

Skeptics often present challenges that test the mettle of even the most seasoned apologist, inviting deeper exploration and understanding. By genuinely listening to these objections, apologists grow in humility and compassion, recognizing the unending journey of faith seeking understanding. Each dialogue becomes an opportunity to witness God's grace working in the lives of both the questioner and the responder, strengthening faith in ways beyond mere human reasoning.

The apologist is called to witness to the faith not just in intellectual arguments but through the lived example of their life. Authentic discipleship acts as a powerful apologetic, demonstrating the transformative power of faith through actions rooted in love, charity, and justice. Apologists must, therefore, align their lives closely with their beliefs, becoming credible witnesses to the profound happiness and fulfillment that come from a life centered on Christ.

In strengthening faith through apologetics, Catholics are reminded that every question or challenge represents an opportunity for grace. When approached with humility and confidence, these encounters reveal this journey's transformative power. Faith becomes not a static set of doctrines but a dynamic, lived expression of truth, hope, and love. In this space, the Roman Catholic faith reveals itself as a wise, compassionate teacher, guiding both heart and mind towards an encounter with the Divine.

Ultimately, the journey of apologetics nurtures a living faith in the participant and reminds the believer that faith, though profoundly personal, is not an isolated endeavor. It flourishes in community and dialogue, enriched by the diverse reality of human experience. As we defend and articulate the faith, we draw closer to each other and to God, united in the shared mission of proclaiming the good news of Jesus Christ.

Chapter 26: Apologetics for the Existence of God

As we delve into the profound subject of the existence of God, it's essential to recognize that this question sits at the very heart of many theological inquiries and philosophical debates. The consideration of God's existence is not confined to the realm of faith alone; it's an issue that has captivated the minds of philosophers, scientists, and skeptics throughout history. For the Roman Catholic apologist, the proof of God's existence isn't merely an intellectual exercise; it's a testament to the truth and beauty of the faith itself.

In approaching the existence of God, we rely on a synthesis of philosophical reasoning, theological reflection, and experiential insight. This triad forms the cornerstone of Catholic apologetics and serves as a guide through the intricate paths of doubt and belief. The challenge lies in articulating these profound truths in a manner that not only addresses the doubts of the skeptic but also nurtures the faith of the believer. It is through this endeavor that we hope to inspire a transformation of the heart and mind.

Philosophical arguments for God's existence have been pivotal in Catholic apologetics, providing a rational foundation upon which one can understand the divine. Among these, the classical proofs—often attributed to the likes of Saint Thomas Aquinas—stand as intellectual monuments that have withstood centuries of scrutiny and debate. These proofs include the Five Ways: the argument from motion, causation, contingency, degrees of perfection, and the teleological argument or the argument from design.

The argument from motion posits that everything in motion must have been set in motion by something else. If we trace this back, seeking a first unmoved mover, we arrive at the necessity of a primal force that initiated everything without itself being moved. This unmoved mover, Aquinas argues, is what we call God. Such reasoning appeals to the principle of causality, a fundamental intuition that underlies much of human reasoning.

Similarly, the argument from causation asserts that nothing can cause itself. Every effect must have a cause, and if we follow this causal chain back to its origin, we encounter the necessity of a first cause, an uncaused cause. This, Aquinas argues, we also call God. The leap from philosophical reasoning to theological recognition is one that acknowledges both the limits of human understanding and the transcendent nature of the divine.

The argument from contingency points out that things in the universe come into being and pass out of it. Thus, there must be some necessary being, one that contains within itself the reason for its existence, something not contingent upon anything else. This necessary being, as Aquinas posits, is God. In theological terms, God is described as self-existent and eternal; qualities that affirm His necessary nature.

Aquinas' fourth way, the argument from degrees of perfection, observes varying degrees of qualities such as goodness, truth, and nobility in the world. These degrees imply the existence of a singular pinnacle, a perfect being embodying these qualities to the highest degree, which we understand to be God. This perspective not only affirms God's existence but also enriches our understanding of God as the source of all that is good and true.

The final of Aquinas' ways—the teleological argument or the argument from design—finds evidence of intelligence in the order and purpose seen in the natural world. Such design appears far too intricate to be attributed to chance. From the laws of physics governing the cosmos to the complex structures of biological organisms, this argument stands as a testament to a grand designer, whom we call God. Contemporary developments in science have only deepened this sense of wonder and inquiry.

Apart from Aquinas, other philosophical arguments, such as the ontological argument proposed by Saint Anselm, offer unique insights into God's existence by asserting that God, being a perfect being, must exist in reality because existence is a perfection. However, this argument has sparked extensive debate and remains a point of contention among philosophers.

While philosophical arguments offer substantial ground, they must be complemented by theological reflections and personal experience. Faith is not merely an intellectual assent but a lived experience, permeating every aspect of life. The Resurrection, the sacraments, and the lived witness of the saints reveal a God who is not only a philosophical principle but a personal presence in the world.

For the skeptic, who dismisses these arguments as mere abstractions, we propose an exploration of the intrinsic yearning within the human heart for meaning and purpose. This desire, which transcends material satisfaction and temporal achievement, points towards a reality that fulfills our deepest aspirations, echoing Saint Augustine's poignant reflection that our hearts are restless until they rest in God.

It's crucial to address the role of faith, which, while informed by reason, transcends it. The mysteries of faith invite us into a relationship with God that is both rational and experiential. It is here that we encourage a personal encounter with the divine, an invitation to witness God's presence in prayer, the sacraments, and the community of believers. This encounter is transformative, offering a glimpse into the love and grace that define the Christian experience.

In engaging with those who doubt or deny the existence of God, the apologist must embody patience, humility, and love. It's through genuine dialogue and an earnest sharing of the Catholic faith that the barriers of disbelief can be overcome. We must remember that belief in God is not coerced but gently nurtured through understanding, relationship, and witness.

Ultimately, the apologist's task is not to merely convince with arguments but to invite others into a journey of discovery. In this journey, the reason meets faith, and the heart finds its true home in the mystery of God's love. Through this, we fulfill our calling to bear witness to the truth, goodness, and beauty inherent in the divine, affirming that the existence of God is not only a matter of belief but a profound reality that shapes our very being.

Chapter 27: Apologetics for the Divinity of Jesus Christ

In the revelation of Christian doctrine, the divinity of Jesus Christ unfurls as both cornerstone and mystery. Its implications permeate theology, ethics, and personal faith. To engage in apologetics for Christ's divinity is to walk in the footsteps of countless theologians who have sought to illuminate this sacred truth. This chapter endeavors to equip you, the apologist, with a nuanced understanding and persuasive arguments to demonstrate the reality of Jesus as both fully divine and fully human—a truth that lies at the heart of the Catholic faith.

The very concept of the Incarnation, God taking on flesh, is revolutionary. It elicits wonder and demands rigorous intellectual engagement. The Gospels, the primary source documents of Jesus' life and claims, provide a potent starting point. Within their narratives, Jesus repeatedly identifies Himself with the Father, performs divine acts, and accepts the worship due only to God. Consider, for instance, His assertion in the Gospel of John: "Before Abraham was, I Am" (John 8:58). This statement is not just a temporal claim but an echo of the divine name revealed to Moses at the burning bush. Jesus doesn't merely claim prophetic or messianic authority; He assumes the very identity of God, a claim that would be blasphemous if not true.

Yet, Jesus' divinity is not merely a matter of self-assertion. His divine authority is substantiated by miraculous works. The Gospels document healings, exorcisms, and most poignantly, the resurrection. These miracles are not mere displays of power but signs pointing towards the transcendent nature of Christ. Take the healing of the paralytic in Mark 2:1-12, where Jesus not only heals physical infirmity but, more provocatively, forgives sins—a prerogative that belongs to God alone. In forgiving sins, Jesus makes an implicit claim to divine authority, a claim validated by His miraculous power to heal.

The resurrection stands unparalleled in its significance as the capstone of Christ's divine identity. The event is so pivotal that Paul the Apostle famously writes, "If Christ has not been raised, then our preaching is in vain and your faith is in vain" (1 Corinthians 15:14). The resurrection vindicates Jesus' divine claims and establishes Him as the living Lord. Historical apologetics has combed through the accounts of the resurrection, underscoring its plausibility and attesting to the immediate and profound impact it had on His disciples. Their willingness to face persecution and martyrdom hinges on their conviction of having encountered the risen Christ—a transformative experience that affirmed His divinity beyond doubt.

Beyond scriptural and historical analysis, the divinity of Christ invites philosophical reflection. The anthropological consequences of the Incarnation are profound. By becoming human, God ennobles the human person, offering a bridge between the finite and the infinite. The divine/human interface in Christ suggests a model of perfected human existence, one in which divine grace elevates human nature without obliterating it. This union, called the hypostatic union, is a mystery that compels the human intellect to grapple with the compatibility of divinity with humanness, encouraging us to appreciate the salvific significance encompassed in this union.

The Nicene Creed, one of the touchstones of Catholic faith, encapsulates the Church's understanding of Christ's divinity. Formulated in response to early heresies, it affirms Jesus as "God from God, Light from Light, true God from true God, begotten, not made, consubstantial with the Father." The language of the Creed serves as a bulwark against any reduction of Jesus to mere prophet or teacher. To recite the Creed is to align oneself with a long tradition of faith that proclaims Jesus as co-eternal and co-equal with the Father, setting Christianity apart from any philosophical or religious system that withholds divinity from Him.

As Catholic apologists, we are tasked not only with defending these tenets but also with articulating them in a manner that resonates with contemporary audiences. This involves engaging with modern objections that question or reinterpret the divinity of Christ, ranging from secular skepticism to religious pluralism. One must dissect these perspectives with respect yet firmness, demonstrating the internal consistency of the doctrine of Christ's divinity and its indispensability to the coherence of Christian faith.

For instance, the challenge posed by secular humanism, which often denies any supernatural reality, necessitates a reinvigorated dialogue grounded in historical and existential authenticity of the Christ event. Moreover, within the context of interreligious dialogue, the divinity of Jesus is a point of distinction and discussion. Yet, by emphasizing Christ's unique salvific role, without disparagement to other beliefs, one can foster a dialogue that seeks understanding rather than confrontation.

Finally, the personal dimension of encountering the divinity of Jesus can't be understated. Faith, while rational, is an engagement of the whole person. Inviting others to encounter the living Jesus through prayer, liturgy, and personal witness allows them to connect with His divinity not only intellectually but existentially. This approach aligns with the Catholic tradition, which values both reason and experience as pathways to divine truth.

In summation, apologetics for the divinity of Jesus Christ stands as a cornerstone of engaging both the mind and heart in the journey of faith. This chapter provides not only the intellectual tools required for such a defense but also encourages a holistic approach that integrates scriptural fidelity, theological rigor, philosophical inquiry, and personal witness. Through this multi-faceted approach, one can confidently present Jesus Christ as God incarnate, the source of divine love, and the ultimate Revelation to humanity.

Chapter 28: Apologetics for the Authority of the Catholic Church

The authority of the Catholic Church stands as a pivotal foundation for understanding its teachings, practices, and its historical influence on the world. The role of authority within the Church is not merely a matter of hierarchy or discipline; it is rooted in profound theological truths and a deep historical continuity that connects believers across centuries. The Catholic Church claims a unique authority, derived from its apostolic foundation, which requires thorough exploration and defense, especially in an era where authority is frequently questioned.

To discern the basis of the Church's authority, one must look back to its inception. Christ's commission to Peter, often termed the "rock" upon which the Church would stand, is a central scriptural foundation. In Matthew 16:18-19, Jesus's declaration to Peter forms a cornerstone for the Church's understanding of authority, investing Peter with keys, a symbol of administrative and spiritual authority. This Petrine foundation is not solely historic but remains intensely relevant as it upholds the unity and infallibility principles that Catholics believe are essential for the faith's purity and consistency.

It is crucial to underscore the Church's claim to apostolic succession, a concept asserting that today's bishops, through an unbroken line of ordination, possess the same authority conferred upon the apostles. This lineage is not an abstract theological construct; rather, it's an organizational and spiritual reality that ensures the continuity of the teachings and sacramental validity. The Church teaches that this apostolic authority is perpetuated through the magisterium, comprising the pope and bishops who guide the Church in matters of faith and morals.

While many Christian denominations acknowledge some form of church authority, the Catholic Church's understanding is comprehensive and unique. This claim to authority is not an exercise of power for its own sake but a service to truth and the faithful. Here lies a significant apologetic challenge: explaining how this authority operates as a means to maintain unity in truth for Catholics worldwide while respecting the individual's conscience and freedom. This balance between authority and freedom often raises questions, especially from those who advocate for a personal interpretation of faith outside institutional guidance.

An essential aspect of the Church's authority involves its teaching office, or magisterium, which interprets Scripture and Tradition. This function is essential because it offers a definitive guide amid the multiplicity of interpretations that can arise. The magisterium serves as a guardian against the flux of subjective interpretation that can lead to relativism, ensuring that the Church's doctrine remains consistent with its foundational truths. The Church's authority is thus seen as both protective and directive—guarding the deposit of faith while guiding the faithful in understanding complex theological truths.

The doctrine of infallibility, notably, is central to understanding this authority. Defined dogmatically during the First Vatican Council in 1870, papal infallibility ensures that when the pope speaks "ex cathedra" on issues of faith and morals, he is preserved from error by the Holy Spirit. This dogma often generates misunderstandings, requiring apologists to clarify its scope and significance, emphasizing that infallibility is not omniscience or arbitrary power but a gift to the Church for maintaining doctrinal fidelity.

The historical context of the Church's authority reveals its resilient adaptability and profound consistency. Through councils, such as Nicaea and Trent, and in response to heresies and reformations, the Church exercised and refined its authoritative roles. This historical perspective provides a rich system for apologists, illustrating the Church's continuous effort to articulate and defend the faith amidst varied challenges. The Church's ability to navigate these challenges while maintaining its core teachings is a testament to the authority it claims—a blend of divine guidance and human stewardship.

Moreover, the Church's authority extends into ethical and social realms, providing moral guidance on pressing issues like bioethics, social justice, and economic systems. This moral authority, while derived from theological and philosophical principles, also draws its legitimacy from the Church's historical role as a mediator of divine values in a changing world. The Church's teachings on these matters remind us that authority, in Catholic understanding, is integrally linked to the pursuit of the common good and the protection of human dignity.

An apologetic appeal to the authority of the Catholic Church must confront objections rooted in both historical events and contemporary experiences. Scandals and abuses within the Church have led many to question its moral authority. Apologists must engage these realities honestly, recognizing human failure while pointing to the enduring truth and beauty of the Church's teachings despite its members' imperfections. The ability of the Church to reform and renew itself speaks to the divine grace underpinning its authority.

Ultimately, the Church's authority is expressed most profoundly through its capacity to inspire and enact a vision of human flourishing as envisioned by Christ. Apologetics must not only defend this authority but demonstrate its richness and necessity for a cohesive, developed faith capable of addressing the complexities of modern life. Engaging skeptics and seekers requires showing how the Church, through its authoritative voice, can offer answers and hope in a fragmented and often disillusioned world.

Therefore, the apologetics for the authority of the Catholic Church involves more than a defense of institutional hierarchies; it is an invitation to explore a profound communion that transcends time and culture, aiming to unite humanity in truth and love under the auspices of divine authority. Through understanding this authority, believers and skeptics can find a pathway to deeper engagement with the Catholic faith, revealing a worldview that is both ancient in its roots and dynamic in its expression.

Chapter 29: Apologetics for the Moral Teachings of the Church

Moral teachings are, in essence, the lifeblood of the Church's guidance for its faithful. They offer not just a pathway to personal holiness but also form a blueprint for a just and compassionate society. Yet, this is precisely where many skeptics find themselves at odds with the Church. How can a centuries-old institution claim to hold the keys to a moral compass relevant to today's complex issues? Apologetics, particularly in the realm of moral teachings, seeks to answer these questions and defend the truths upheld by the Church.

Before proceeding with defending these teachings, it's essential to identify their roots. The Church's moral teachings are not arbitrary edicts handed down by ecclesiastical authorities; they are deeply anchored in both natural law and divine revelation. Natural law—the understanding of morality inherent to human reason—serves as a universal foundation recognized across diverse cultures and religions. Coupled with divine revelation, it forms the moral bedrock upon which the Church builds its theological edifice. While natural law offers principles discursively discerned by reason, divine revelation presents them in a light illumined by faith, which is deemed clearer and more authoritative.

An essential aspect of defending the Church's moral teachings lies in addressing misconceptions. Critics often argue that these teachings are outdated or irrelevant, especially in a world championing individual autonomy. Yet, moral relativism, where ethical truths are perceived as subjective, poses a danger by undermining the idea of universal truth. The Church stands firm not just for the sake of tradition, but out of a conviction that objective moral truths are discernible and necessary for human flourishing. Here, the apologist must emphasize the coherence and universality of moral teachings, drawing parallels between the consistency of the Church's doctrines and the innate moral intuition found across mankind.

Moving deeper into specific moral teachings, one may look to the Church's teachings on issues like human dignity, family, and social justice, which serve as perennial areas of moral engagement. The Church's stance, though often counter-cultural, aims to uphold human dignity against myriad threats, whether through its teachings on life ethics—from conception to natural death—or its advocacy for the sanctity of marriage and family life. These teachings present a compassionate yet firm defense of the inherent worth present in every human life and the fundamental social structures that nurture it.

The skepticism about Church teachings on sexual morality perhaps garners the most attention. In this battleground, apologetics must carefully differentiate between the perception of repression and the reality of self-giving love that these teachings encourage. In a culture that often equates freedom with license, the Church posits love as genuine freedom—a call to will the good of the other and a challenge to elevate desires toward virtuous ends. The apologist must demonstrate how living according to these teachings leads not to self-denial, but to authentic human fulfillment.

Other areas of moral teachings, such as those concerning economic justice and care for creation, reflect the Church's commitment to addressing systemic moral issues affecting the global community. Here, the Church calls for a prophetic witness against structures of sin, bearing witness to the Gospel's liberating power. It is within these teachings that the apologist can dialogue with the wider world, affirming the Church's role in advocating for social and environmental justice by appealing not only to faith but to shared human values.

Inevitably, some may challenge the Church's moral credibility by pointing to instances of moral failure by its members. These are painful truths, but they don't invalidate the Church's teachings. Instead, they highlight the timeless call to return to these moral truths with renewed vigor. Acknowledging these failures should not deter the apologist; rather, it should spur earnest efforts to embody and advocate for the integrity of these teachings.

Furthermore, moral apologetics benefits from a broader philosophical engagement, drawing from existential, ethical, and metaphysical discussions. For instance, the relationship between freedom and responsibility, or individual conscience and communal good, are not solely religious inquiries but resonate within the broader philosophical discourse. By showcasing the harmony between Church teachings and sound philosophical reasoning, the apologist not only defends these teachings but illustrates their compelling rationality.

Ultimately, the task of apologetics for moral teachings is not merely to protect or justify; it aims to inspire, to call to higher moral striving, and to engage in patterns of life rooted in truth and love. The Church's moral witness, when genuinely lived, shines as a light in today's often disenchanted world. Apologists must, therefore, embody these teachings personally, becoming living testimonies to the beauty and wisdom of the Church's moral vision.

As with all endeavors of the heart and mind, humility is paramount. Apologists, like their Master, must approach every argument and dialogue with charity and patience, drawing others not by the force of argument but by the attraction of truth lived out. In doing so, the moral teachings of the Church will continue to not only weather the storms of skepticism but flourish as guiding lights in an ever-complex world.

Chapter 30: Apologetics for the Sacraments and Their Efficacy

The sacraments stand as visible symbols of grace, instituted by Christ Himself to sanctify humanity. To fully grasp their place within the framework of the Catholic Church is to appreciate their role as sacred vessels conveying divine grace through physical means. In an era where spiritual realities are often overshadowed by materialism, the sacraments offer tangible assurances of divine intervention and mercy. They serve not only as rites of passage within the Church but as perpetual reminders of God's unwavering love and presence.

Understanding these sacred rites requires both an appreciation of their historical context and a grasp of their theological underpinnings. The sacraments are not merely symbolic gestures; they are efficacious signs instituted by Christ that produce grace ex opere operato. This means it's not the holiness of the minister or the recipient that effects the grace; rather, it is Christ working through the sacrament. Herein lies their divine efficacy, an idea central to Catholic sacramental theology.

To scrutinize the sacraments without considering their divine origin and function within the Church is to devolve into mere ritualism. Catholic theology teaches that the sacraments are essential means of sanctification, woven into the fabric of human life by Christ Himself. The Council of Trent reaffirmed their necessity, countering Reformation critiques by asserting both their origin in divine will and their role in human salvation.

Time and again, skeptics challenge the sacramental system, often arguing that grace need not be bound to specific rites or rituals. However, the Church holds that the sacraments are the ordinary means by which God dispenses His grace. This distinction is crucial and not about limiting God's power but about following God's chosen method of sanctification. Each sacrament was instituted for a particular purpose, reflecting the manifold ways in which God attends to the spiritual needs of His people.

Take, for example, the Eucharist, considered the source and summit of Christian life. When Christ declares, "This is My Body" and "This is My Blood," He invites believers into an intimate communion that transcends time and space. Transubstantiation may perplex the modern mind bound by empirical evidence, but it calls for a faith that acknowledges a reality beyond what is immediately perceivable.

Theological discourse often encounters debate over whether the sacraments could be deemed superstitious or unscientific. Addressing such critique involves delving into the realm of sacramental economy, wherein physical elements—water, bread, oil—become conduits of spiritual grace. This paradigm is not to be viewed as mere magical transformation but as a mystery that operates under divine ordinance. Catholic scholars have long held that sacramental efficacy relies on Christ's promises rather than the faithful's understanding or the minister's sanctity.

It's important to recognize the sacramental economy's roots in the Incarnation. In becoming flesh, Christ sanctified the material world, making it a fitting vessel for divine grace. The sacraments, then, are extensions of this fundamental act, allowing Christ's redemptive work to reach every corner of human experience, thereby providing both sanctification and renewal.

Critics often posit that the sacraments dilute faith by placing emphasis on ritual. Yet, the sacraments are designed not to compete with faith but to bolster it. They are encounters with the divine that engage the whole person—body and soul. For the skeptic, this may seem redundant or unnecessary; but for the believer, the sacraments provide an avenue for deepened faith and spiritual growth.

When we speak of baptism, it carries the promise of new life and purification from sin, not just symbolically but through the actual conferral of grace. Confirmation strengthens the baptized with the gifts of the Holy Spirit and prepares them for the full life of Christian discipleship. These sacraments of initiation, particularly when viewed through the lens of apologetics, bring a richness and depth to the Christian journey that mere rhetoric cannot convey.

Next, the sacrament of reconciliation serves as a vital element of the Church's ministry of healing. Through confession, the penitent is not merely reciting sins but participating in a sacramental encounter with God's mercy and forgiveness. Analyses of confession within apologetic frameworks often emphasize its psychological and spiritual benefits, highlighting its role in cultivating humility and self-awareness.

Holy Orders and Matrimony illustrate the sacraments' vocational dimension, underscoring the Church's commitment to service and community life. These sacraments structure the life of the Church, empowering individuals to live out their calling in meaningful and transformative ways. They are, in essence, commitments to God that reverberate through personal and communal existence.

The sacraments of healing—Reconciliation and Anointing of the Sick—specifically address human frailty and suffering. In particular, Anointing of the Sick fortifies the ill and prepares the dying, reminding believers of the hope and comfort offered by a loving God. These sacraments call believers to a profound trust in God's ultimate plan, inviting participation in the paschal mystery of Christ.

In apologetics, it's crucial to communicate that the sacraments are not isolated acts but part of a coherent and unified ecclesial tradition. Apologists must, therefore, not merely offer a defense but cultivate an understanding and appreciation for these sacred rites in the broader context of Church teaching and practice.

Ultimately, the apologetic endeavor surrounding the sacraments is one of faith seeking understanding. It invites both the skeptical and the devout to explore the profound depths of God's grace manifested through these sacred actions. A robust defense of the sacraments champions both their antiquity and their enduring relevance, affirming them as gifts from

Christ, entrusted to His Church for the sanctification of the world. Far from being archaic remnants of a bygone era, they offer a timeless bridge between the divine and the human, an invitation to partake in the mystery of God's love continually unfolding in our lives.

Chapter 31: Apologetics for the Role of Mary and the Saints in Catholic Theology

The veneration of Mary and the saints holds a uniquely revered position within Catholic theology, often met with curiosity and misunderstanding from other Christian traditions. Catholic theology does not worship Mary or the saints as divine. Rather, it acknowledges them as important intercessors, guiding individuals towards a closer relationship with God. This chapter examines the theological basis for their veneration, emphasizing their roles not as competitors to God, but as profound witnesses to His glory.

At the heart of understanding Mary's role is the concept of theotokos, which means "God-bearer" or "Mother of God." This title, affirmed at the Council of Ephesus in 431 AD, highlights Mary's singular role in salvation history: she bore the Incarnate Word. Her willingness to accept God's plan, uttered in the words "Let it be to me according to your word" (Luke 1:38), exemplifies perfect obedience and faith. For Catholics, emulating Mary's servitude becomes a model for personal holiness, as she embodies the ultimate commitment to God's will.

The communion of saints, a cornerstone of Catholic understanding, underscores the interconnectedness of the Church's members—living and deceased. Saints represent the triumph of faith over worldly afflictions, affirming the possibility of holiness despite human frailty. This communion reflects a familial bond, where those perfected in grace assist the living through intercession, much like how one would ask a friend to pray for them.

To defend the role of saints, one must delve into Scripture and Tradition. The Bible frequently depicts the righteous praying for one another, such as in Revelation 5:8, which describes heavenly beings presenting prayers before God. Furthermore, James 5:16 encourages believers to "pray for one another" for efficacy. These scriptural foundations affirm the Catholic conviction that those closest to God in heaven can effectively intercede on behalf of the living.

Protestant critics often argue that the veneration of saints detracts from Christ's mediating role. However, Catholics maintain that such veneration is not a replacement for the worship due to God alone. Instead, it is an acknowledgment of the saints as partners in the divine mission, who reflect God's light into the world. Their lives are testimonies of divine grace triumphing through personal struggle and fidelity to Christ.

Mary's exemplary virtues pave an apologetic path to understanding her vital role. Unlike any other human, she is venerated as sinless from her conception—an assertion defined as the Immaculate Conception. This dogma, articulated by Pope Pius IX in 1854, provides a lens through which Catholics view salvation: Mary is preserved from sin not by her merit, but as a singular grace from God in preparation for her role in the Incarnation. The theology surrounding Mary centers on her unwavering faith and unique participation in Christ's redemptive work.

In ecclesial tradition, the saints serve as fragrant witnesses to Christ's transformative power, displaying how ordinary lives can resound with sanctity. Through earthly sufferings and joys, they highlight the spectrum of human experience viewed through a lens of divine fidelity. St. Therese of Lisieux's 'Little Way,' for instance, reveals holiness in small daily acts done with great love, echoing the universal call to sanctity.

The saints also function as spiritual mentors. Stories of the saints have nurtured generations, offering examples of steadfast faith amidst trials. This mentorship extends beyond worldly demise, as Catholics believe the saints intercede on behalf of those on earth, elevating human petitions to the divine throne. This interaction embodies the profound hope that echoes in Hebrews 12:1, where the "great cloud of witnesses" surrounds the faithful, encouraging perseverance.

Criticism often arises regarding the extent of Marian devotion. Some suggest that it borders idolatrous practices. However, in genuine Catholic practice, Marian devotion seeks to honor her role in the divine plan, recognizing her as the foremost disciple of Christ. The Rosary, a common devotional prayer, contemplates the mysteries of Christ's life through Mary's perspective, unifying Christological meditation with Marian intercession.

Moreover, understanding the saints as intercessors transforms the human relationship with the divine. Instead of demanding immediate access to God in solitude, believers are invited into a heavenly family, underlining God's relational aspect. This analogously mirrors how earthly families work together to nurture, support, and guide one another towards shared goals—the ultimate being communion with God.

In defending these beliefs, Catholic apologetics relies on a comprehensive synthesis of Scripture, Tradition, and Reason. The interplay of these sources fortifies the theological assertion that Mary and the saints, far from obscuring Christ, illuminate His light. They stand alongside believers, pointing consistently to the heart of the Gospel: salvation through Jesus Christ.

Such veneration does not diminish Christ's role as the sole Redeemer. Instead, it illuminates the manifold ways His grace operates through His creation. Through the lives and prayers of Mary and the saints, Catholics find models of holiness, tangible signs of God's redeeming love, and assured advocates for their earthly and spiritual needs.

Ultimately, understanding the role of Mary and the saints requires recognizing the rich quilt of the Church's history, woven with lives dedicated to manifesting the Gospel anew in each generation. Their stories, steeped in faithfulness and grace, act as perpetual reminders of God's kingdom—both anticipated and experienced.

In the final analysis, Catholic theology's inclusion of Mary and the saints enriches the faith, underlining the significance of community within the divine plan. As Catholic apologists address critiques and questions, they invite dialogue back to the invigorating truth at the heart of the Church: the relentless and transformative love of God, made manifest through His creation, ever guiding humanity into deeper communion with Him.

Chapter 32: Apologetics for the Bible and its Interpretation

As we venture into the complexities of Biblical apologetics, we encounter a multifaceted endeavor that seeks to affirm not only the validity of Scripture as the Word of God but also its rightful interpretation within the Roman Catholic tradition. The Bible, a divinely inspired text, stands as the foundational pillar of Christian teaching and doctrine. However, it requires careful exegesis to unveil its truths without falling victim to misinterpretation or manipulation. Here, we aim to articulate a defense for both the authenticity of the Biblical texts and the interpretative framework employed by the Catholic Church.

One critical aspect of defending the Bible involves establishing its historical reliability. Many skeptics question the authenticity of the Biblical narratives, suspecting them to be embellished tales. Yet archaeological discoveries and historical research consistently affirm the Bible's credibility. The Dead Sea Scrolls, for instance, offer a glimpse into the textual consistency of the Old Testament across centuries. The Church Fathers, in their intellectual rigor, understood the significance of such findings and engaged with contemporary evidence, affirming how rational inquiry fortifies faith.

The interpretative task of the Church is to discern the spiritual and moral truths embedded in Biblical narratives. This endeavor is no mere academic exercise but a profound journey into divine revelation. The Catholic Church, guided by the Holy Spirit, has maintained that Scripture is to be read within the "symphony" of Tradition. This sacred Tradition encompasses the teachings of the Apostles and the continuous testimony of the Church. It guards against subjective interpretations and ensures that the message remains consistent with the core tenets of the faith.

In defending the interpretations, one might ask, "Why is the Church's perspective privileged over personal interpretation?" The answer lies in the role of the Magisterium, the Church's teaching authority. Christ entrusted His Apostles and their successors with the keys to His Kingdom, embedding the Church with a responsibility to teach and guide the faithful. This authority is not an imposition but a custodianship of faith, ensuring interpretations are not swayed by transient cultural or personal biases.

A robust apologetic of the Bible also involves addressing apparent contradictions and resolving doctrinal differences that arise from varying interpretations. Catholics maintain that Scripture, though divinely inspired, was written by human hands in specific historical contexts. Understanding the human author's cultural and historical backdrop allows for a deeper appreciation and resolution of these seeming contradictions. Harmonization and synthesis, rather than fragmentation, lead to a coherent and holistic understanding of Scripture.

Moreover, the spiritual dimensions of the Bible cannot be ignored. Beyond legalities and historical accounts lies a rich confluence of allegory and symbolism, meant to speak to the soul and spirit. Saint Augustine wisely noted that Scriptures contain depths that surpass human wisdom. Thus, spiritual reading, illuminated by prayer and reflection, becomes an essential practice, enabling believers to see beyond the literal to the eternal truths that underpin the Catholic faith.

In addressing those skeptical of Biblical interpretation within Catholicism, it is important to underscore the unity between Scripture and Tradition. For the Church, these are not separate streams but a single river flowing from the heart of God's revelation. Tradition does not obscure the Scriptural message but rather enlightens and enhances it, providing a living context for its understanding.

Furthermore, the Catholic approach does not eschew scholarly inquiry but embraces it. Historical-critical methods, linguistic studies, and literary analysis offer valuable insights that enrich understanding. The Church encourages and participates in academic dialogue, confident that truth—whether historical, scientific, or theological—cannot contradict, for all truth is of God. Faith and reason are not adversaries but allies in the quest for understanding God's Word.

In summary, the apologetic task for the Bible and its interpretation within the Catholic tradition is a dialogue of faith seeking understanding. It is not a rigid imposition of dogma but a dynamic and living engagement with the divine mysteries. Apologists are called to articulate this harmonious relationship between Scripture, Tradition, and Reason, demonstrating a vibrant faith fully alive in the world today. As Roman Catholics, we are entrusted with the joyful responsibility of sharing this understanding with a world searching for truth and meaning.

Conclusion

As we reach the conclusive threads of this exploration, it becomes ever so clear that the Roman Catholic tradition, with its intricate relationship of theology, philosophy, and apologetics, offers not just a faith, but a way of living deeply in tune with the human condition. Over the chapters, we've journeyed through the richness of Catholic Social Teaching, navigated the delicate balance of virtues and vices, and fortified our understanding with the powerful goods of faith exemplified through the sacraments and doctrines. What stands out is not simply the robust theological scaffolding of the Church but its innate ability to meet the profound needs of the human spirit.

The Roman Catholic Church, in its sturdiest arguments and most foundational beliefs, impresses upon the heart a distinct compassion. This compassion is visible in its emphasis on the dignity of the human person and its commitment to social justice. The Church stands as a guardian of these teachings, challenging society to uphold the worth and sanctity of every life. This promotion of dignity is not just a doctrinal assertion but a lived reality, calling scholars and believers alike to reflect it in every action.

Catholicism's call to solidarity and the promotion of the common good beckons us to look beyond ourselves, encouraging a collective responsibility that transcends individualism. It invites us into a dialogue that is not always comfortable but necessary, forging communities that mirror the divine love inherent in the Trinity. The Church's social doctrine is not a mere catalogue of teachings but a living testament to a faith deeply engaged with the world.

For skeptics contemplating the threshold of faith, consider the historical and philosophical depth the Church holds. The evidence supporting the divinity of Jesus Christ, the profound writings of early Church fathers, and the thoughtful engagement with science and reason, reveal a faith not at odds with intellectual rigor but in harmony with it. It is this harmony that positions Catholic thought as a beacon for those searching for truth amidst the chaos of conflicting ideologies.

Moreover, the sacramental life, laden with grace, offers a tangible encounter with the divine. Each sacrament unfolds a unique aspect of the divine mystery while grounding believers in the practical and mystical presence of God. Through them, the faithful are continually invited to participate in God's grace, transforming each moment of life into a sacred offering to the Creator.

In considering the virtues, both theological and cardinal, one recognizes the Church's insight into human behavior and ethics. These virtues do not simply guide moral actions but nurture the soul towards holiness. They remind us that virtue is an interior journey and communal responsibility, urging every faithful to embody truth, courage, and love in a fragmented world.

As for Mary and the saints, they form an illustrious gallery of witnesses, embodying the potential for holiness in human life. Their lives offer a model for contemporary believers, demonstrating that sanctity is not only achievable but desirable. They inspire the faithful to aspire to a life of dedicated service, surrender, and joy.

In articulating the Catholic faith, apologists are called not just to defend, but to invite. The dialogue we encourage with skeptics and seekers must always be rooted in understanding and love. By engaging deeply with their questions and objections, we cultivate not only stronger arguments but more profound relationships. This evangelistic mission is not about winning debates but sharing the transformative truth of the Gospel.

In summary, the purpose of this handbook is not only to equip apologists for intellectual and practical engagements but to illuminate the heart of a faith that seeks to transform every facet of human existence. The Roman Catholic Church, in its timeless wisdom and ever-relevant teachings, offers hope—a hope that persists through trials, endures through doubts, and ultimately leads to the embrace of divine love. Thus, as we close this volume, let us renew our commitment to live out these truths with fidelity and vigor, ever eager to share the richness of our faith with the world.

Appendix A: Appendix

In the ever-expanding journey to articulate and defend the Roman Catholic faith, this appendix serves as a vital overlay—a compilation meant not as the final word, but as a comprehensive guide for deeper exploration. The task of Catholic apologists is to navigate a world that often misunderstands or challenges foundational doctrines, thus requiring a robust repertoire of resources to bolster their defense. Herein, we compile key texts, ecclesiastical documents, and insightful works by theologians who have tread this path before, lighting the way with their wisdom and profound understanding. This resource list encompasses the rich dialogue of Catholic teaching, history, and apologetic discourse, offering scholars, theologians, and even skeptics a well of knowledge that supports both academic inquiry and spiritual edification. As the mysteries of faith call for both heart and intellect to engage fully, this appendix invites its readers to delve into the depths of Roman Catholic thought with renewed vigor and enduring hope.

Comprehensive Resource List

For those who seek to deepen their understanding of the Roman Catholic faith and enhance their skills in apologetics, a substantial body of resources exists. This list aims to provide a guide that is both broad and insightful, capturing the richness of Catholic thought across history, theology, philosophy, and practical application.

A foundational element of Catholic learning is the **Scriptures**. The Bible serves as a primary source of divine revelation, doctrinal understanding, and apologetic strength. It's beneficial to have several versions, such as the Douay-Rheims, Revised Standard Version Catholic Edition (RSV-CE), and the New American Bible (NAB) for comparative study. Alongside these, *The Catechism of the Catholic Church* offers a structured synthesis of Catholic doctrine and should be considered essential reading for apologists.

Turning to **historical texts**, the writings of the Church Fathers provide indispensable insights into early Christian thought and the formation of doctrine. Works by Saints Augustine, Athanasius, and Iranaeus, available in collections like *The Ante-Nicene Fathers* and *The Nicene and Post-Nicene Fathers*, anchor the faith historically and offer rigorous theological exposition. For a comprehensive understanding of the development of Church doctrine and its application, John Henry Cardinal Newman's *An Essay on the Development of Christian Doctrine* is a timeless resource.

Philosophical thought has always been enmeshed with Catholic theology. *Summa Theologica* by Saint Thomas Aquinas is a pillar of Catholic philosophical writing. It challenges readers to delve into profound questions about God, ethics, and human nature, integrating reason with revelation. The insights of G.K. Chesterton in books like *Orthodoxy* and *The Everlasting Man* provide stirring apologetic arguments and delightful prose, demonstrating that reason and faith are not adversaries but complementary allies.

You'll also find modern apologetic techniques in texts like Peter Kreeft's *Handbook of Christian Apologetics* and Karl Keating's *Catholicism and Fundamentalism*. These works address contemporary questions of belief and practice, providing concise, articulate defenses of Catholic doctrines against secular and Protestant critiques.

Exploring the intersection of **science and faith** is crucial for any Catholic apologist facing modern skepticism. Resources like *Faith and Science Reconciled* by Dr. Stacy Trasancos and the work of Father Robert Spitzer in *New Proofs for the Existence of God* illuminate the compatibility and complementary nature of scientific inquiry and faith.

For those interested in exploring **Catholic social teaching**, which is woven through chapters of this volume, key documents include *Rerum Novarum, Gaudium et Spes*, and *Laudato Si'*. Each encyclical not only elucidates Catholic ethical teachings but also provides directives for living out these principles in the modern world.

Art and literature embody the cultural dimensions of the faith. Dante Alighieri's *The Divine Comedy* offers a poetic journey through Christian cosmology, while Flannery O'Connor's stories challenge readers with their profound moral and theological insights. These works highlight how the Catholic imagination shapes understanding of the divine, human suffering, and redemption.

For **digital resources**, there are numerous avenues to explore. The Vatican's website offers a plethora of documents, speeches, and teachings from the Popes. Online courses and lectures at institutions such as the Augustine Institute provide robust platforms for delving deeper into theological education and apologetics.

Engaging with contemporary Catholic thinkers and discussions is essential. Podcasts like *Catholic Answers Live* and *Pints with Aquinas* offer engaging dialogues on faith issues, inviting scholars and skeptics alike to explore profound questions in an accessible format. In parallel, blogs and forums such as *Strange Notions* foster community and discussion among those interested in the intersection of faith and reason.

An effective resource list wouldn't be complete without highlighting the power of prayer and liturgical life as nourishment for the apologetic endeavor. The *Liturgia Horarum*, or Liturgy of the Hours, imbues daily life with the rhythm of prayer, fostering strength and wisdom in articulating the faith.

In compiling this Comprehensive Resource List, aimed at Roman Catholic scholars, theologians, and skeptics alike, the intention is to equip individuals with the breadth and depth necessary for dialogues with the modern world. These resources, harmonizing ancient wisdom and contemporary insights, are vital in crafting robust, compassionate, and compelling defenses of truth. The landscape of learning is wide, yet rooted deeply in the timeless truths that the Roman Catholic Church stands upon, truths that call to all of humanity in every age.

www.ingramcontent.com/pod-product-compliance
Lightning Source LLC
Chambersburg PA
CBHW081937160726
47999CB00008B/2427